Money *for* Life

Budgeting Success
and Financial Fitness in Just 12 Weeks!

Steven B. Smith

A **Kaplan Professional** Company

Vice President and Publisher: Cynthia A. Zigmund
Acquisitions Editor: Mary B. Good
Senior Managing Editor: Jack Kiburz
Interior Design: Lucy Jenkins
Cover Design: DePinto Studios
Typesetting: Elizabeth Pitts
Graphic Design: Jennifer Streiff and David Anderson

Published by Dearborn Trade Publishing
A Kaplan Professional Company

Printed in the United States of America

04 05 06 10 9 8 7 6 5 4 3 2 1

Library of Congress Cataloging-in-Publication Data

Smith, Steven B., 1966-
Money for life : budgeting success and financial fitness in just 12 weeks / Steven B. Smith.
p. cm.
ISBN 0-7931-8793-1 (6 × 9 pbk.)
1. Finance, Personal. 2. Financial security. I. Title.
HG179.S55134 2004
332.024–dc22

2003026598

This book is dedicated to those who have
a dream to pursue,
the vision to plan,
the courage to run,
the expectation to perfect,
and the persistence to win!

Advance Praise for *Money for Life*

"The beliefs, habits, and behaviors of the characters whose stories are told in *Money for Life* are something we can all relate to and learn from. Achieving long-term financial freedom is not complicated, but it takes discipline and effort. Make the 12-week commitment to live by the principles of this book. This is the first step in financial planning, and it can change your life!"

—Sheryl Garrett, CFP, Founder, The Garrett Planning Network, Inc., and Author, *Garrett's Guide to Financial Planning* and *Just Give Me the Answer$*

"Steven Smith's unique storybook approach in *Money for Life* to teaching sound budgeting principles is truly different from anything I've ever read. I was immediately drawn in to the real-life characters, who show the reader how to put into practice the principles that make budgeting really work. The 12-week course was easy to follow and can be done by anyone. I very much recommend this book."

—James P. Christensen, Ph.D., Author, *Rich on Any Income*

"*Money for Life* effectively captures the essence of solid budgeting principles and provides readers with excellent online tools for taking charge of their finances. I highly recommend this system."

—Judy Lawrence, Budget Coach and Author, *The Budget Kit: The Common Cents Money Management Workbook*

"Hundreds of books have been devoted to personal finance. *Money for Life* stands alone. In it, you will find not only all the fundamentals of proven money management skills but also the tools you will need to implement these principles in your life and begin to profit immediately."

—Ryan W. Christiansen, Financial Advisor and Vice President, McDonald Financial Group

Contents ■

List of Figures ■

■ CHAPTER 2

■ CHAPTER 3

■ CHAPTER 4

■ CHAPTER 5

■ APPENDIX B
Choosing an Envelope Budgeting System

■ APPENDIX C
Using Variable Income with an Envelope Budgeting System

■ APPENDIX D
Reference Material

■ APPENDIX E
Mvelopes® Personal: An Envelope System for Today's World

Acknowledgments

Truly great and rewarding projects do not happen without the vision, motivation, and support of talented people. Such has been the case with *Money for Life.* I am grateful for the assistance and support of many people without whom this project would not have become a reality.

Particularly, I am grateful to:

- Warren Rosner, Nicholas Thomas, Richard Kuhn, David Neddo, Brett Palmer, David Leeper, Michael Krieger, and the rest of the In2M management team. Your collective vision, passion, hard work, and outstanding support from day one have aided in the creation of a truly great organization focused on helping individuals reach their financial fitness potential.
- The In2M employees who work tirelessly every day to make visions and dreams become a reality for our customers.
- My business partners and In2M shareholders—without you and your continued support, this project would not have been possible.
- My editor, Mary Good, and the rest of a very qualified and professional organization at Dearborn. Your insight, energy, passion, and dedication to this project have been extraordinary. Thank you for making this project both a success and a great pleasure.
- Alex Lubertozzi and Jennifer Fusco with Prologue Publishing Services—for their insight and creativity in lending form to this idea. Thank you for giving me some latitude while helping to create a manuscript that was true to our original vision. Your continued support and guidance have been amazing.

- To my parents, Ron and Gloria, who have always been great supporters of me and this project. The positive impact of your continued prodding, encouragement, and enthusiasm should not be underestimated. May you enjoy the greatest that life has to offer as you begin the rewarding next stage.
- Finally, to my family, for their unbelievable love and support. You have always been there and it has always made the difference. And especially to my wife, Jana, for an extraordinary journey, the likes of which could only have been experienced with you at my side. May life be as awesome for you as you have made it for me.

Preface

During the Great Depression, my grandparents, like many people at that time, found themselves in a very difficult financial situation. After moving to find employment, my grandfather worked hard to provide for the basic needs of his family. After receiving income for a few months, my grandfather again was in a very tough situation when the mill he worked for was forced to close. Several months behind on rent, in debt, and struggling to make ends meet, my grandparents moved back to the city where they had lived before.

When they arrived in Portland, Oregon, my grandfather looked for work and finally secured a position with a machining company. At that time, he and my grandmother had little to nothing. With steady employment, my grandparents set out to create some financial security. They adopted a cash envelope system of budgeting, and started living cautiously within their means. Each time my grandfather received a paycheck, he and my grandmother would plan their spending and divide their income between a number of envelopes labeled for each category of spending. When they wanted to purchase a major item, money was set aside in advance. When they decided to build a house, they saved the money for the lot and, once purchased, built their modest home as they were able to secure the needed materials.

My grandparents did not live a lavish lifestyle, but they always had the money they needed to do what they wanted. Later, when my grandfather retired, he and my grandmother were able to continue doing the things they wanted to do. My grandfather died many years ago, but the financial resources he and my grandmother were able to set aside in both savings and investments continue to support her increased financial needs—she now requires more assistance in her later years. Never once have her children been required to assist her financially, and she still has the financial resources to support her needs for years to come. My grandparents lived the timeless principles contained in this book and were financially fit as a result.

Contrast this story with that of my other grandparents. Born and raised during the same period of time, they too struggled during the Great Depression. However, their life was one of constant financial struggle, living paycheck to paycheck. When my grandfather died several years ago, my grandmother had few financial resources to meet her needs. For many years, her children had to assist her with the resources necessary to maintain her care.

Both sets of grandparents had modest incomes. However, the financial outcomes they achieved later in life were very different. While we may believe our financial choices will impact only us, clearly, choosing poor financial fitness can have a lasting impact on our immediate loved ones and our extended families.

These stories, together with many others, inspired my wife and I to adopt the envelope budgeting system soon after we were married. Many years have passed, and I have seen these simple, yet timeless principles positively impact my family and the lives of countless others. Ultimately, these success stories proved to be the motivation to develop a modernized envelope budgeting system for use in today's world. A CD facilitating a free 30-day trial of that system is included inside the back cover of this book.

This book was written to provide the vision, education, and motivation necessary for anyone of any income level to successfully adopt these time-tested financial principles. The story told within these pages is about a couple dealing with the complexities of managing personal financial resources in our society today. Their success can be your success as you adopt the principles they discovered through the wisdom of an experienced financial advisor.

My grandfather's life was a simple one, yet he was rich, because he always had the financial resources he needed to do what he wanted. Way to go, Oz, you will always be an inspiration to me.

Introduction

We live in a society driven by financial excesses. Unfortunately, the compensation for this lifestyle is often poor health, debt, or even the demise of the family. While the 1990s were arguably one of the most prosperous decades in history, collectively we are pursuing a course that could ultimately leave us financially destitute. Total consumer debt in the United States exceeds $1.8 trillion. In the early 1990s, according to the Economic Policy Institute based in Washington, D.C., average household debt was a staggering 80 percent of annual net income. Today, that number has grown to an unbelievable 109 percent. Not surprisingly, the number of those now seeking protection from creditors through personal bankruptcy is also growing at an alarming rate.

The resulting stress has severely impacted families. Studies show that financial issues remain a significant cause of contention in homes and one of the greatest contributors to divorce. While many of us may not directly experience personal bankruptcy or broken homes, far too many people are making choices daily that have the potential of bankrupting their financial future and destroying their ultimate happiness.

The good news is that despite the worrisome financial dynamics of our complex society, there are tools available to help reverse—or altogether avoid—the downward cycle of debt, daily financial stress, and frustration.

The goal of this book is to show you how you can become the master of your finances now and for a lifetime. With the explosion of new technologies over the past 20 years, we have found more and more ways to spend our money that remove us from the immediate impact of our actions. The problem is, despite the added convenience these technologies have ushered in, we still have to live with the consequences of our spending. *Money for Life* illustrates, through the fictional story of Ryan and Christine Richardson, how we all can use the principles of an envelope budgeting system, and how technology can improve, rather than erode, our awareness of the money we're earning, spending, and saving on a monthly, weekly, and even daily basis.

The story told in these pages focuses on one specific family. But the situations, issues, and conflicts could arise with almost any family in any circumstances–at any age, in any part of the country, and at any income level. Therefore, the lessons learned and solutions put into practice by the people in this story will apply to anyone who is having trouble keeping expenditures under control.

By putting this information in the context of a story, you will be better able to identify with, understand, and relate to the problems and issues described. To highlight the principles embodied in the storyline, a section called "Applied Principles" has been included at the end of each chapter. These sections will break down and explain what is going on in the characters' financial situations, and how they were able to use the principles of envelope budgeting and the new tools available to get their financial houses in order.

By combining a very typical story of financial difficulties with a clear explanation of the principles used to solve the problem, *Money for Life* can change the way you look at your money, and how you plan for your future and, ultimately, your life.

Prologue

Ryan and Christine Richardson once enjoyed a happy, carefree relationship. They are both college educated, make a good combined income, and are focused on successfully raising a family. As they and their family have grown, so have their responsibilities–they've experienced the joys of parenthood and owning a home, as well as the trials, tribulations, and headaches that come with them. They have never been particularly good at managing their finances or living within a set budget, but have always managed to get by. It hasn't been until recently that the situation has become intolerable, making it impossible for them to ignore it any longer. Like so many couples in their predicament, they have allowed financial stress and frustration to erode their happiness.

The following profiles provide relevant background information on Ryan, Christine, and the other characters involved in their story:

RYAN RICHARDSON

Ryan Richardson is a 35-year-old senior project manager for Medical One, a company that produces custom software for the medical industry. He manages several projects over the course of a year and is known for his ability to complete projects on time and under budget. Although he finds tracking–and mercilessly cutting–costs at his job natural, he has a much harder time putting this kind of thinking into practice in his personal life. He grew up in the small town of Lake Worth, Florida. His father made a good living as a sales rep for an industrial equipment company, and his mother worked at the town's only travel agency. While they enjoyed spending, his parents always seemed to struggle to make ends meet, and family finances were a constant source of contention. He met Christine while they were students at the University of Florida, and they married a year after graduation. They had their first child, a son named Chad, four years later, and a daughter named Jennie three years after that. Five years ago, Ryan completed his MBA degree after four long years of night school. It enabled him to get his current job at Medical One, but caused him and Christine to incur more debt in the form of a student loan. Ryan has always enjoyed spending money—"That's what it's there for" is his motto. He tends to purchase on impulse, buying the newest and most up-to-date technology. While he has never really been able to live within a budget in his personal life, Ryan always felt an obligation to be the family's provider and make the significant financial decisions.

■ CHRISTINE RICHARDSON

Christine Richardson is a 35-year-old elementary school teacher. She grew up in New Jersey and attended college at the University of Florida, where she met Ryan. Although she grew up in an affluent household—her father was a prominent attorney, and her mother ran the household and participated in numerous charity events—she never learned much about personal finances. Her parents were quite conservative about spending money, but never discussed financial matters with Christine while she was growing up. As a result, Christine tends to worry more than Ryan about spending too much money, despite the fact that she has never had a good grip on how much is too much. When she and Ryan were first married, they both worked—Christine as a third-grade teacher at a neighboring community's elementary school and Ryan as a sales rep for a medical supplies firm. From the time that Chad was born up until a year ago, Christine stayed at home to raise the children. Chad is now 8 years old, and Jennie is 5. When Jennie entered an all-day preschool last year, Christine resumed her teaching career, this time getting a position as a fourth-grade teacher at an elementary school across town. At first, she was thrilled at the idea of returning to her profession, doing what she loves, and bringing home an extra income. Although she still loves teaching her nine-year-olds, she's bewildered by how, with all the extra money they now earn, they seem to have less money than ever and are getting even more into debt.

■ ROB GOLDMAN

Rob Goldman is a 36-year-old senior programmer for a networking software developer. He works in a highly competitive field and is very good at his job. Having worked at his company since graduating college, he's advanced into management and makes a good salary. Rob met Ryan at the University of Florida, where they were roommates, and has been friends with Ryan ever since. He married Susan, his high school sweetheart, while they were still in college, and they had their first child, Megan, shortly thereafter. Megan is now 14 years old and has a little brother, Danny, who is 8. Although Rob, like Ryan, has always felt responsible for the financial decisions of the family, he is also the one who worries more about money. He used to be much more on top of his family's finances, but since moving up in his job, he has taken on ever more responsibility at work, spending more and more time at the office. He grew up in a blue-collar family in which both of his parents had to work to make ends meet. He worries about the looming costs of college for their daughter, Megan, and about how they're going to ever put anything away for their retirement.

■ SUSAN GOLDMAN

Susan Goldman is a 35-year-old homemaker who takes an active role in her community's activities and social scene. She grew up in the same town as Rob and dated him her last two years in high school. She attended the University of Georgia, where she could still be relatively close to Rob. Susan has always been an extremely energetic, social person. It was in college where she first got into trouble with using credit cards. Always wanting to participate with her friends in going on trips, buying clothes, and having nice things, she maxed out three credit cards by the end of her sophomore year, and had to have her parents bail her out with a loan. She was careful with her credit cards after that, but as Rob moved up in his company, Susan felt more relaxed about spending money on the things she wanted. She loves feeling financially independent, and will sometimes lie to Rob about the cost of purchases she's made because she knows he would get mad if she were to be completely honest with him. Although she and Rob have known each other for most of their lives, they rarely have discussions about money and budgeting. It was not something they ever talked about before getting married, and it's only been a source of friction since. As a result, they tend to avoid the subject until it becomes a crisis.

■ SHIRLEY CHANG

Shirley Chang is a 32-year-old administrative assistant working for a financial services firm owned by Tom Maxwell. She is a single mother of two boys—13-year-old David and 9-year-old Sam. She and her husband, Russell, divorced four years ago, and although he's tried to keep up with the child support, he's been laid off from two jobs in the past few years. After they separated, Shirley had to go back to work. And although she earns a good living working for Tom, she found out early on how tough it was financially trying to raise two children on her own. Shirley has been using an envelope budgeting system recommended to her by her boss, Tom, for the past three years. She met Christine and Ryan Richardson five years ago when her son Sam and the Richardsons' son Chad were in the same preschool. Shirley became good friends with both Christine and Ryan soon after. Whenever they could, they would pitch in to help each other with the children, and Shirley and her boys have become a regular fixture in the Richardsons' home most weekends for brunch and to spend time together.

■ JOHN AND PATTY RICHARDSON

John and Patty Richardson are the parents of Ryan Richardson and live one town over from their son and his family. John, who has been a sales rep in the industrial equipment business for close to 40 years, is nearing retirement. Patty stayed at home to raise Ryan and his brothers and has enjoyed the perks of working as a travel agent since the boys moved out of the house. Neither John nor Patty has ever kept to a budget on a sustained basis. They did manage to put some money into investments for their retirement, but most of that went into mutual funds that have not performed well for them. Having grown up in the 1940s, John took on the role of financial decision maker in the household. Patty, although more of a saver than John, never felt as though she should voice her concerns about their finances and always took a backseat to her husband when it came to money. John and Patty still take frequent trips and feel that they deserve to splurge on themselves. On top of their spending habits, they still have a substantial amount of debt from car loans, their home mortgage, and credit cards. They are approaching retirement with much trepidation at the thought of having to live within a fixed income or continue to work.

■ WALTER AND LUCY HOWARD

Walter and Lucy Howard are a retired couple living comfortably in the home in which they raised their five children. Walter, who was a technician at the power plant, and Lucy, who was a librarian, both have been retired for a little over ten years. Both grew up during the latter days of the Great Depression and always felt conscious of holding onto their money, as they knew it could all be lost in an instant. They still use a traditional envelope budgeting system and have for more than 30 years. Today, they have a tremendous net worth because of the spending principles that enabled them to save and thus make investments in stocks, bonds, and real estate. They were one of Tom Maxwell's first clients back in the early 1970s and have been with him ever since. Their use of an envelope budgeting system enabled them to get out of debt and turn their finances around. They are now able to enjoy their retirement, planning trips to see their grandchildren or taking cruises without having to wonder whether or not they can afford it.

■ TOM MAXWELL

Tom Maxwell is a certified financial planner who has been working with individuals and families to plan their financial futures for more than 30 years. Because he works with so many families, he knows that the key to having a secure financial future is being able to keep expenditures in line with income. He's made it his mission to help people first figure out how to stick to a budget, and then figure out what to do with the money that's left over.

■ ■ ■ ■ ■

While Ryan and Christine and all the rest of our cast are fictional characters, the financial dilemmas they face are based on the true-life experiences of many people. And like our protagonists, many are finding that there really is a way to regain control and successfully manage their finances in today's society. This book was designed for those seeking a blueprint for achieving long-term financial fitness. Here are just a few of the benefits financial fitness can bring:

- As you take your next vacation, you know that it is completely paid for before you leave.
- The next time a major appliance needs to be replaced, you have the money already set aside.
- You never need to worry about checking the account balance at the bank before you pay a bill.
- You look forward to making decisions regarding the education of your children, because you are actively saving money for this purpose.
- You spend time planning and anticipating retirement, because you are debt free and prudently investing money to fund the lifestyle you want to have.

Chapter One

The Final Straw

The stores were filling up with frantic shoppers. With only four days until Christmas, people were buying last-minute gifts and decorations with little regard to practicality . . . or price. Christine and Shirley were battling the toy store crowds with great enthusiasm. Shirley carried a few boxes in her arms while she attempted to help her friend guide an overloaded cart through an aisle bursting with bright pink.

"Jennie's only five years old," gasped Christine. "Why does her *doll* need a $40 plastic minivan?"

Shirley smiled. "I'm glad David has outgrown that I-need-it-now stage. I'm still working on Sam. Of course, now all they want are video games and DVDs. Come to think of it, I know I'm spending more this season than I ever did when they were little. Maybe I should be envious."

"Oh, I don't think you have anything to be jealous of, Shirley. I still can't believe that you're nearly done with your Christmas shopping and you haven't overspent your holiday budget. Plus, I still have to worry about sneaking the gifts from Santa into the house, not to mention the woes of spelling tests, swimming lessons, junior high, dating . . . "

"You're right, you're right. I'll have to remember to remind you how easy you have it once Chad becomes a teenager."

"Touché," Christine laughed. "I guess the stress never stops, does it?"

Just as the cart was about to overflow, Shirley dragged it to a miraculously open cash register. She placed her items on the counter, removed some cash from a red-and-green envelope, and handed the bills to the clerk. Christine started unloading her loot onto the conveyor.

"Speaking of stress," she continued while Shirley picked up her change and purchases, "how am I ever going to fit all this stuff into the car?"

"Weren't you talking about getting a new SUV?"

"You mean, other than the one I'm buying for Jennie?" Christine teased. "Actually, since Ryan just got a raise, we were thinking about it. Things are going really well for him over at Medical One. And, since I started back to work, it feels like we're finally able to afford things. It was really tight this summer, though. And you know Ryan, he loves having the latest and greatest."

Christine handed over her credit card and waited to sign her name on the receipt. The cash register whirred and whirred. The young girl behind the counter formed her face into a pout. "I'm sorry, ma'am, but do you have another card? Your MasterCard doesn't seem to be working."

"No problem," Christine said with a weak smile, as she handed over her Visa card to the girl. "Sorry about that, this one should work."

"I'm sure it's not your card. It's probably our computer—I think it's just exhausted after this crazy day."

She took Christine's credit card and turned back to the register. Christine stood, tapping the pen against countertop. Shirley started packing the bags and boxes back into the cart. The register whirred again. Still, a receipt did not appear.

The clerk turned back to Christine, and handed her Visa card back to her. "I'm sorry, ma'am, but it's saying your card is declined."

"Could you please check it again? I know there's nothing wrong with the card."

"Let me call my manager over," the girl said, avoiding eye contact.

"What's going on?" asked Shirley.

"I don't believe this," said Christine, getting exasperated. "I know we have plenty of money left on that card. I really don't need this right now." Shirley patted Christine on the arm as the manager walked past a long line of anxious customers.

"Is there something I can help with?" the manager, a man a few years younger than Christine, asked.

"I can't get her card to work," the girl said. "I don't know if it's the machine or what."

"Can I have your card, ma'am?" the manager asked.

If one more person calls me "ma'am," Christine thought, *I'm going to scream.*

The manager ran the card through again and waited. After whirring for a minute, the machine stopped and displayed the words CARD DECLINED. He handed the card back to Christine and said, "I'm sorry, but, for whatever reason, it's saying your card is declined. Do you have another card you could use?"

Christine cringed, knowing that the one card she did have left probably wouldn't have enough on it to cover the purchase. But her only alternative was to write a check she was sure they couldn't cover, and she wasn't about to do that. "Um, well," she said, digging back into her purse with shaking hands, "I do have a store credit card that I think should work." She found the card and turned to Shirley, saying, "I don't like to use it that often, but I guess we can make allowances today." To her great relief, the card went through, although she wasn't sure how. *Did the store raise our credit limit?* she wondered.

Back in the car, with the day's packages loaded in the trunk and seats behind them, Christine wondered what Shirley must be thinking. Here her friend was, single with a child nearly in high school and one in fourth grade, and she was still able to pay cash for all of her Christmas gifts. *Shirley always seems to have it together,* Christine thought. She always knew how much she could spend and, yet, she did not seem worried at all about the looming costs of college. Christine thought about all the expenses she had yet to pay before Jennie and Chad grew up—Chad was only eight years old, and Jennie was just in kindergarten. Their family was so young, and they were earning two incomes *How could this have happened?* Christine dropped Shirley off in front of her new, tidy bungalow. As she backed out of the driveway, she tried to calm herself down. She called Ryan on her cell phone to see if he knew anything about why their cards weren't working.

■ ■ ■ ■ ■

Ryan looked at the clock on his desk. It was 5 PM. With Christine and the kids on Christmas break, they should be home now. He couldn't wait to give Christine the good news. It had been a good day at Medical One, a company that developed custom software for the medical industry. Ryan, as the senior project manager, had delivered his projects on time and under budget. As a result, senior management had approved a $2,000 year-end bonus on top of his recent 6 percent raise for the coming year. Ryan's salary would now top $64,000 a year. It was great news. He felt even better about the Christmas gift he had bought for the family. Maybe he would surprise them with it a few days early. They could celebrate the good news together. He reached for his bag.

Suddenly the phone rang. It was Christine, calling from the car.

"Hi, honey," she said, trying to control her emotions. "I was doing some Christmas shopping and the strangest thing just happened: neither our MasterCard nor our Visa card worked. I know that I haven't paid one of them yet—I was going to pay some bills tonight—but I thought the Visa would be OK. I'm just a little shaken. Do you know what could have happened?"

Ryan sighed and leaned back in his chair. He had charged the family's gift on the Visa card, since it wasn't one Christine used very often. He hadn't told her about it yet, but he didn't think it would be a problem. He had to wonder, though, why on earth the MasterCard was declined.

He started to explain, hoping not to lose his Christmas cheer. "Well, Christine, I was hoping it would be a surprise, but I did put a gift for the family on the Visa card yesterday."

Christine paused. She knew Ryan's gift-giving habits were extravagant, but he did just get that raise. He couldn't have charged *that* much. *There must have been an error with the Visa company,* she thought. "OK, well, before I sit down to do the bills, can you tell me what you bought? I'm going to have to call Visa and see if our number has been stolen. I'll need to tell them how much was on the card already."

Ryan didn't want to blow the surprise, but he also doubted there was a stolen number or an error with the credit card company. "Well, it wasn't cheap, but I know I didn't exceed our limit. We were only carrying about $3,000 on the Visa, according to the last bill. And I didn't think you were using that card. Did you make any purchases with it?"

Christine stiffened. "Well, I've had to do most of the Christmas shopping myself," she said, a little defensively, "and you know I needed a new coat."

"So how much have you charged on it?" Ryan asked.

"I don't have the exact total in my head, Ryan," she snapped. "But I didn't think it was going to be enough to max out the card. I thought we had more on the MasterCard, too, but apparently we didn't."

Ryan winced, remembering that he'd put his new golf clubs on the MasterCard.

"Somehow, between your big gift and my other shopping," Christine said, "we've maxed out the Visa as well."

The silence on both ends lasted for what seemed like an eternity.

"So how much *did* you spend?" said Christine finally. "And *what* did you get?"

"The important thing is I thought this gift would be something the whole family could enjoy," Ryan said, forcing himself to sound happy. "I bought us a 36-inch HDTV. Merry Christmas, honey. *Honey?*"

The line went dead.

■ ■ ■ ■ ■

Christine picked up Chad and Jennie from the babysitter's house and headed home.

What are we going to do with a new TV? she wondered. *And how are we ever going to get on top of our finances if we don't even discuss major purchases together?*

Before the raise and Christine's return to work, she and Ryan knew that the strain of living paycheck to paycheck was wearing on their relationship. It seemed no matter how much money he made or how hard they tried to save, they could not get ahead. Christine had loved teaching before she had had Chad and decided to stay at home. She did not regret that she and Ryan had opted to live on only one income, but she did miss her job and the money it provided. Two years ago, however, they had maxed out all their credit cards and sought relief in a home equity loan. At first, they had felt liberated from so many payments, but gradually their credit card balances had returned—the only difference was that *now* they had a home equity loan to pay off as well. With Ryan's career taking off and Jennie now in school, Christine figured that the money she would make back at teaching could be used for some of the "extras" they used to worry about buying before.

She was less upset about the television itself than she was about Ryan's decision to keep it from her. While Christine handled the day-to-day finances, Ryan focused more on the long-term decisions that guided them financially. After all, that's what he was doing so successfully at Medical One. How was Christine supposed to have any control over the checkbook if Ryan didn't tell her everything she needed to know?

Back at home, and with the kids settled in the family room after a light dinner, Christine sat at the kitchen table and tried to make sense of their credit accounts. She totaled the checks she had written and then carefully recorded her most recent check from the school. She sat there, staring at the statements in her hand. Tears welled in her eyes with the realization that they couldn't even cover the minimum amount due to MasterCard before the payment deadline.

It was only two years after the home equity loan and their cards were maxed out again. She was going to have to make a late payment, because they just didn't have the money. Christine thought of the new television that must be sitting inside the house somewhere. Yes, they could return that, they could forget the plans for the new SUV, they could even cut back on Christmas gifts, again, but where would that get them?

We're right back where we started, she thought, *or worse.*

■ ■ ■ ■ ■

Ryan sat in his car in the driveway, hesitant to go inside the house. He could see Christine sitting at the table, most likely paying the bills and figuring out a way for them to start a new budget. It seemed that she did that every month. Every month they made plans to save and to track their expenses, but it never seemed to work.

How could he successfully manage million-dollar projects at the office and yet never get ahead at home? Why weren't he and Christine out of debt yet? They were both intelligent and had college degrees. They were both earning decent money. Managing it just couldn't be that difficult. But somehow they seemed to replay the same scenarios over and over: she worried about how they spent, and he always reassured her. He had steered them through buying their first and second homes, purchasing their cars and furniture, and making plans for retirement and college savings that they would someday implement.

The burden of debt began to settle on him. Where did it all go? Music lessons, new clothes, school events, pictures, family gifts, vacations—it never ended. Yet, all of these things seemed important, even necessary. His family deserved the best. It was up to him to provide it for them. If they were really in trouble, what more could he possibly do?

This is crazy, Ryan thought as he sat looking at the glowing lights from the windows of his own home. *What am I going to say to Christine? How am I going to fix this?*

He knew that he ought to go inside, but instead he sat there thinking. They had met during his second year at the University of Florida and married three years later. She was an elementary education major. He was pursuing a degree in marketing. Christine's parents still lived in New Jersey, where she grew up. Her father was a successful attorney and partner with the firm Madison, Wilson, and Fisher. Christine's parents were careful with their money—their fixation on their household budget was, Ryan thought, unnatural. But they did dote on their daughter. On her 16th birthday, her father had given her a new car, and when she graduated from high school, her parents had flown her and her best friend to Europe.

Ryan, on the other hand, had grown up in Lake Worth, a small city in southeastern Florida, where his father was a sales rep and his mother was a travel agent. His parents made a good living, but they enjoyed spending what they had, when they had it. The souvenirs they bought on their many vacations alone would probably equal a modest full-time salary. Ryan had relied on a part-time job to get him through his four years of college.

One of Ryan's biggest concerns with marrying Christine was a feeling that he might not be able to provide her with the lifestyle she had been given by her parents. They had talked about it, and she had assured him that material things were not required to make her happy. "Just let me know you care about me—and about my needs. As long as we're working together and can talk things out, we'll be OK," she had assured him.

And that was the thought he took with him as he walked into the house.

■ ■ ■ ■ ■

Christine looked up at Ryan when he walked through the door. She could tell by the look on his face that they were both in the same place. She hated it when they discussed money—they seemed to agree on nearly everything else. What was she supposed to do? She never knew for sure what they could or couldn't afford, and she couldn't stand not being able to offer a solution that worked. Things had gotten so far out of hand that she was more confused than anything else.

"I'm sorry," she said. "I just wish that we could be more honest about the situation we're in."

"Oh, honey." Ryan pulled her into his arms. "I know you've been trying to figure this out for a long time. I guess I just thought that this gift would make you happy."

They sat down across from one another at the table, and Christine reached for Ryan's hand.

"I actually do have good news tonight," he said, "so we can celebrate something after all." He told her about the meeting with senior management and the $2,000 bonus.

"That's wonderful," exclaimed Christine. "It will help." She handed him the statements and the latest round of unpaid bills. He studied each item in front of him and came to the frightening realization that he had no easy answer to their predicament. Suddenly, as he sunk down in his chair, he felt the overwhelming pressure that had brought Christine to tears a few hours ago. There was no way they could continue on like this for much longer. They were balanced on a very thin financial line, and that line was about to break unless they made some immediate changes.

He looked up from the piles of envelopes and saw Christine staring into the other room. He followed her gaze. After 12 years of marriage, he could imagine what she was thinking. Over the years, they had worked hard as a couple. Graduating from the university; landing good jobs with promising futures; raising two beautiful, bright, energetic children; buying a house and integrating into a new neighborhood—these were the things they had always wanted. Yet, somehow, they had allowed finances to become a major hindrance to their happiness as a family and as a couple.

"Do you recall when we rented our first apartment across town?" she asked.

Ryan smiled. "You found out that you got your first teaching job and rushed out to that place across the street to buy bulletin-board supplies."

"And you went out to celebrate our two-income status by buying a used convertible."

"Our first debt."

They looked at each other. "Well," continued Christine, "aside from that, we were cautious in those days. What happened? Why don't I feel like this is working?"

"We were supposed to have saved a substantial nest egg by now," Ryan said. "Instead, we have $10,000 in consumer debt on top of a mortgage, a home equity loan, a car loan, student loans . . . "

"Ryan, we can barely pay our bills. I'm afraid to even collect the mail tomorrow with the threat of another one showing up. I've already started back at work. How are we going to get more money?"

"Look, Christine, I just need more time. Things are going well at Medical One, and with potential bonuses, I'm sure we can make enough soon to find a way out of this debt."

"But what do we do in the meantime . . . when the bonus you got today runs out?" Christine asked. "Do you think we could qualify for a higher limit on our credit cards now that I'm working?"

"Probably, but more debt? That will hardly help," said Ryan.

"It's just temporary."

"We said that a year ago. In the meantime, we've maxed out two more credit cards. Obviously, if we're still racking up debt and can barely pay our bills, we must be spending more than we're earning."

Christine stared at Ryan. "You're probably right," she said.

He nodded.

"When I last talked to my mother," said Christine, "she mentioned their standing offer to give us money to help with the kids' needs."

"Oh, great," Ryan snapped. "That's the last thing I need right now. I'm sure your dad will be smitten with me even more then."

"Is that what this is all about? Impressing my father?"

Ryan looked away. "I just want your parents to know I can take care of you. I don't want your father to think I can't give you what you deserve."

"What I *deserve?* What does *that* mean?" Christine looked at him with disbelief. "Is that why you insist on buying all these big-ticket gadgets and pricey gifts? Are you just trying to look impressive?"

Christine had oversimplified the problem, but he had to admit that she had hit a nerve. Growing up, many of his friends' families had been in a better financial position than his. Sure, he wore the name-brand clothing and sported the necessary extras that were popular through the years, but deep down he always felt that his friends' parents were different: they could afford what they gave their children. Even when he was little, he guessed that his parents were spending more than they could afford. Ryan's parents never skimped on anything, but the atmosphere of living hand to mouth because of it was more obvious to their children then they could have known. Ryan didn't want his own children to feel the same way, but was he just repeating the habits of his parents? Were he and Christine sacrificing their future financial security on the altar of today's wants and needs?

"Christine, I'm not a psychiatrist. How do I know why I do what I do? We have a financial problem to solve. We just have to find a way to get some control over the situation."

"What is important to me, though," said Christine, "is feeling that we are working together on this."

"And we do work together, at least," Ryan admitted, "most of the time. But it's obvious that whatever we're doing right now isn't working. You know, I think a big part of our problem is we seem to be making our decisions in a vacuum, without knowing the short-term and long-term impact of what we do.

"And when we try to manage our spending, something unexpected always seems to throw us off.

"You know, Christine, as much as I hate to admit it, I think it's time we talked to someone about this. I don't think either one of us has the answer anymore."

Christine looked away, but nodded her agreement. "Ryan, we can't let money keep dragging us down. Let's work to do whatever is necessary to get control of all this. We have so much, and I'm tired of worrying about our finances. I just want things to get better."

Ryan stood up and placed his hands on Christine's shoulders. "So do I."

■ ■ ■ ■ ■

Shirley and her two boys, David and Sam, arrived the next Saturday, as usual, for brunch. Not sure of how it started, the regular weekend brunch with Shirley and her kids had been going on for nearly as long as she had been friends with Christine and Ryan.

Christine was playfully tugging on Ryan's shirt as he mixed up some waffle batter. She dabbed a bit of the batter with her finger and put some on his nose. "Hey!" Ryan said, and tickled Christine's side. Shirley saw them laughing and horsing around as she closed the patio door behind her.

"Wow," Shirley said, "you two seem to be in an extra good mood today."

"It's another beautiful day in the Richardson household," Ryan grinned.

Christine rolled her eyes as she handed her friend a cup of coffee and sat down at the breakfast table. "Yep, I guess we are feeling pretty good," she said.

"Well, what's up?"

"Oh, well, you remember our shopping trip last week, no doubt." Christine said, and Shirley nodded. "Ryan and I finally decided that we're going to do whatever needs to be done to get out of debt. It's just been a little too hand to mouth around here to feel comfortable anymore."

"Good for you," Shirley said. "I think that's a great idea. And, if you don't mind, can I give you a piece of advice?"

Ryan looked up from his newspaper. "Shirley, you're probably the only person who could give us advice on this. You have to be the most financially organized person we know."

"Maybe," she said. "Of course, it always helps to work in the office of a financial advisor. You know, if it hadn't been for my opportunity to work in Tom Maxwell's office, I'm sure I'd still be trying to work eight other jobs just to make ends meet. Aside from what I've been able to pick up from just doing my job, Tom has taught me how to pay off my debt while saving for the future. You should talk to him. I'm sure he could help."

"That's right," said Ryan, "I'd forgotten about your boss, Tom."

"After the divorce, getting a job working for Tom was a godsend," said Shirley. "If anyone could help make sense of your finances, it's Tom. I've been using his system for years now, and it's made a huge difference for me. His approach is different because he believes that people need to develop the foundation to achieve financial success, which he says is good spending management and budgeting. He believes this is an important first step before he advises them about investment plans and other things. Tom does this for a very reasonable fee, because he knows if he can help you at this level, he will keep you as a client and you will work with him when you start making plans to invest the money you are saving."

"If we're really going to change our spending habits, Ryan, we should absolutely talk with an expert," said Christine.

"Well," said Ryan, "I suppose if you think he's a good guy, Shirley, we should at least hear him out." Ryan pulled the to-do list off the refrigerator and added Tom's number to the list. The sooner he and Christine could get things on track, the better.

■ APPLIED PRINCIPLE 1

The financial path we should seek is the path least traveled.

The average American family carries credit card debt of more than $6,500, and, according to a study conducted by *SmartMoney* and *Redbook* ("The Truth about Women, Men, and Money," *Redbook,* November 2003), more than 20 percent of respondents said they were carrying a credit card balance of over $10,000. Astoundingly, in our world today, more than 75 percent of graduating college seniors in America have credit card debt. And even more remarkable, an ever-growing number of high school seniors have credit card debt as well. According to the *Wall Street Journal,* more than 70 percent of Americans live paycheck to paycheck. That means that nearly three-quarters of Americans may be as close as one paycheck away from financial disaster.

These startling statistics represent the personal financial path most traveled, the path of least resistance, the path to financial anemia, the path Ryan and Christine were following. When you take an honest look at your level of financial fitness, what do you see? If you are on the path most traveled, you will see a struggle to make payments on time; a significant credit card and consumer debt load; a lack of emergency savings; little or no measurable savings for handling long-term objectives, such as your children's education; and no real plan for achieving a comfortable retirement. As we tread this well-worn path, we often lull ourselves into a false sense of security: Our society constantly tells us that the path we all are on is taking us in the right direction. Banks and credit card companies allow us to "handle" more debt with the "convenience" of small monthly payments. Advertisements barrage us with the message that our hard work entitles us to an ever-increasing collection of material goods. Society measures success by what we *have* rather than by what we are doing to secure a future.

But focusing on what others prescribe for us can be a dead end. Take an example from nature. There is a funny kind of insect called a processionary caterpillar that feeds on pine needles. These curious insects move through the trees in a long procession, one leading the next, each with its eyes half-closed and its head placed snugly against the rear extremity of its predecessor. The great French naturalist Jean-Henri Fabre was very interested in this insect and spent some time studying its habits. After patiently experimenting with a group of caterpillars, he was finally able to entice them to the rim of a large flower pot, where he succeeded in connecting the first one with the last one, ultimately forming a complete circle. The caterpillars started moving around in a circular procession, which had neither beginning nor end. The naturalist expected that they would eventually tire of their useless march. However, through sheer force of habit, the circle of caterpillars kept moving around the rim of the flowerpot. For seven days and seven nights they kept the same relentless pace and, doubtless, would have continued were it not for complete exhaustion and hunger. Though an ample supply of food was close at hand and plainly visible, it was outside the range of the circle, so they continued along the beaten path. They were following instinct—habit, custom, tradition, precedent, past experience, standard practice, or whatever you choose to call it—but they were following it blindly. They mistook activity for accomplishment. They believed they were following the right path—but they got nowhere.

Financially, have you ever felt like these caterpillars, working hard but getting nowhere? When we fall into this useless circle, we totally neglect our financial potential. For many, it is not until they experience a major financial setback that they look around and really understand that their journey down the financial path most traveled has led them right back to where they started. The good news is that we are not these caterpillars. We can pick our heads up, break the cycle, and make our own path to financial security.

Often in life, the path we should seek is the path least traveled. When you get to the top of a mountain, there aren't many others there—most people are coasting in the by-ways or resting in the valley. Becoming financially fit requires a break from the masses and a discovery of the path to the top. In this book, you will learn about age-old principles that will assist you in managing your own budget and planning for a prosperous future. And much like experiencing the exhilaration that comes from viewing the world from a high mountain peak after a hard climb, you will personally understand the excitement that comes from knowing the path to financial fitness.

■ APPLIED PRINCIPLE 2

Awareness is the first step on the path.

The first step to changing your financial course is to recognize that the direction you are currently pursuing may be a dead end. This realization is often much more difficult than it sounds. While most of us have a general feeling for our level of financial fitness, we are often in a complete state of denial regarding our financial weakness. With the overwhelming availability of consumer credit, home equity loans, and debt consolidation loans, we are able to successfully mask the impact of our overspending and poor financial decisions. This was certainly the case for Ryan and Christine. While we can see our state of physical health in a mirror every morning, most of us have not incorporated such a candid financial assessment program into our daily lives to gauge our financial fitness. Many of us don't see or recognize the need to make crucial changes until life–or creditors–has dealt us a significant financial blow.

Now is the time to recognize the need for change. Chances are very good that if you're reading this book you see a need to rethink your financial habits. To add clarity to your general thoughts, candidly answer the following questions:

- Do you carry over balances on your credit cards from month to month?
- Have your credit card balances increased year after year?
- Have you participated in a home equity loan or debt consolidation loan in the past three years for the purpose of paying off consumer debt, only to have consumer debt return?
- Do you schedule the payment of monthly bills around the receipt of your paycheck?
- Do you pay your bills and take care of all monthly expenses before you determine an amount for savings?
- Have you used credit cards or charge accounts to fund major events or purchases during the year, including holiday spending and vacations?
- Do you make major purchases based on the amount of a monthly payment rather than a cash purchase price?

- Have you borrowed money to purchase an automobile and then purchased a different one before the previous vehicle has been paid for?
- Do you constantly monitor your bank account balance to make sure you are not bouncing checks?
- Has a lack of proactive planning and mutual financial decision making led to arguments and frustration within your relationship?

If you answered yes to any of the above questions, you are very likely following the masses. Ryan and Christine were headed in this direction before they finally recognized it was getting them nowhere. Coming to this realization is the first step to achieving true financial fitness.

■ APPLIED PRINCIPLE 3

Sincere desire is the second step on the path.

The battle to become physically fit is waged and won in the mind *before* it is waged and won in the gym. Likewise, the battle to become financially fit is fought in mental terms before it is fought in terms of the checkbook. Real change always starts from the inside. Sincere desire fuels the engine of change; without it, sustained change cannot occur. To gauge your level of conviction, ask yourself what you would like to change most about your current financial situation. Are you tired of having money control your life? Has financial stress and decision making become a source of significant contention and frustration in your relationship? Do financial worries seem to upend the happiness associated with every other aspect of your life? Does the burden of debt limit your ability to do the things you would like to do? Are you constantly concerned about how you will find the resources to retire comfortably?

If you truly desire to change your financial course, you will not waste time with avoidance tactics, such as complaining about your situation or making excuses for past behavior. You cannot rewrite history—dwelling on previous mistakes and placing blame will only keep you focused on the negative.

Sincere desire will keep you thinking of the positive, looking forward to a future that is free of financial burden. The greatest poverty is the poverty of desire. Ultimately, no one can help you until you've decided you're ready for it.

The decision to make a real change can be stressful, even painful. Ryan and Christine discovered this, but then had the courage to seek advice that could help them change the course of their financial fitness. For them, sincere desire proved to be the difference between wishful thinking and motivated, proactive effort.

■ APPLIED PRINCIPLE 4

Becoming truly committed is the first obstacle to real change.

Winston Churchill said, "It is no use saying, 'We are doing our best.' You have got to succeed in doing what is necessary." In order to succeed in doing what is necessary, you need to follow the process of commitment. This requires the following three steps.

STEP 1: Write it down.

The first step is to actually write down the things to which you are committing. What are the specific areas you would like to improve? These could include:

- No longer living paycheck to paycheck
- Reducing or eliminating consumer debt
- Saving for long-term spending requirements, including retirement
- Being able to travel without going into debt
- Paying cash for your next vehicle purchase
- Having money set aside for emergencies
- Creating and living within a budget
- Only purchasing those things you can truly afford
- Working together with your spouse to achieve financial goals
- Eliminating the fear, uncertainty, and doubt surrounding financial management
- Having the peace and happiness that comes from knowing you are financially fit

There are many other financial goals worthy of personal commitment. The goals you write down at this stage will help you focus your efforts proactively as you learn about other important principles surrounding overall financial fitness.

Most couples who are financially fit have applied the principle of becoming committed and facing financial fitness obstacles together. Without the commitment of both parties, it is often impossible to move forward in a positive way. As is the case with Ryan and Christine, most couples come from vastly different financial backgrounds. And, often, the environment you grew up in is the primary contributor to your attitudes toward money.

While it is often not easy to get on the same financial page, it is very important. You can start by finding common ground surrounding the financial issues that are causing friction, frustration, stress, or the avoidance of proactive financial planning. From there, you can move to developing mutually important financial goals. Finally, it is important to agree to work together to achieve these goals. One person pulling the other along eventually will become tiresome and prove frustrating. Two people pulling in the opposite direction will both give up and quit altogether. However, two people pulling in the same direction have a high likelihood of successfully achieving their goals. When Ryan and Christine finally made a mutual decision to change direction, they started making progress toward finding real solutions.

STEP 2: Properly prepare by making a list of obstacles that may get in your way.

True commitment will always be tested by the unexpected. No matter how well you plan, something unexpected will inevitably arise. At these times, the truly committed will keep going in their planned direction, while others will sit down and seek an easier path. One of the keys to successfully navigating the tough spots is to make a list of the obstacles that may steer you away from financial fitness. This way, you will be better equipped to climb over or avoid them altogether. Anticipating these obstacles is not easy, but if you take a good look at past experience, you can successfully determine most of the pitfalls. These may include unexpected events, temptation to keep up with the purchasing habits of neighbors and coworkers, or invitations to participate in unplanned social outings or travel. As was often the case with Ryan and Christine, these can upend your progress and knock you off track. By listing these obstacles, you can prepare mentally to address them as they arise. It is a rocky reality that you will be less able to meet commitments until you have prepared reasonable contingencies to cope with all possible obstacles.

STEP 3: Make it happen.

True commitment propels you to action. Ralph Waldo Emerson said, "We can have anything we want. All we have to do is pay the price and take it." Well-directed persistence based on proper planning will combat any degree of aimlessness. Sometimes, worthwhile things come easily, but they usually require dedicated and consistent effort. In the case of achieving true long-term financial fitness, there are no quick fixes and no magic pills. However, if you are truly committed, you can follow the path that Ryan and Christine will follow, and in as little as 12 weeks, you can be well on your way to reaching your financial goals. Now is the time to get started.

■ APPLIED PRINCIPLE 5
Be prepared to change your thinking.

Albert Einstein once said, "The significant problems we face cannot be solved at the same level of thinking we were at when we created them." If you want to become financially fit, you need to be prepared to think differently than you have in the past. You have to be prepared to look at things differently than society does.

If you are prepared to adjust your thinking, you will begin to see solutions where before you only saw problems. You will be able to learn from the experiences of others–both good and bad. As you follow Ryan and Christine in their quest to become financially fit, you will learn many things that may represent alternate views from those with which you are familiar. Ultimately, you must be prepared and willing to incorporate new thinking into your financial life. As you do, you will make substantial progress toward becoming financially fit.

Chapter Two ■

A Bold Move

The New Year started for Ryan and Christine with a great deal of financial insecurity hanging over their heads, and yet they were looking forward to the future more than they had in quite a while. Perhaps it was overcoming their mutual fear of discussing their finances with each other, or maybe it was the fact that Shirley had provided a tangible lead by referring them to her boss, a capable financial advisor.

Whatever it was, Ryan had marked down in his day planner a reminder to call Tom Maxwell on January 2, right after the holidays. He hated to think of their newfound resolve to get their financial house in order as a "New Year's resolution"—how many of those had he made and broken in his lifetime? But he felt that he and Christine had turned a corner. They had come to the realization that they could no longer continue to spend as they had. But, he also knew they needed a system that would work with their way of life. When they had tried different approaches in the past, they always ended up like fad diets—they worked for the first few weeks, but eventually, old habits would drift back and they would be right back where they had started, only deeper in debt. Hopefully, Shirley's boss would be able to show them a better way than what they'd already tried.

When Ryan called Tom Maxwell's office during a morning break, he heard Shirley answer the phone.

"Tom Maxwell's office," she said.

"Hey, Shirley," said Ryan. "I'm following up as we discussed on Saturday. We want to try and set up an appointment with Tom."

"That's great, Ryan!" Shirley said. "If you guys are able to come in next week, he has availability Wednesday at 2:00 or Thursday at 4:00."

"I think Thursday afternoon will work best. Can you pencil us in?"

"Sure," she said. "Hold on a moment, Ryan, and I'll put Tom on so you can talk over your situation with him."

"Thanks a bunch, Shirley."

Tom Maxwell, a certified financial planner with more than 30 years' experience helping individuals and families build their nest eggs and secure their financial futures, was a down-to-earth, gregarious man. He believed in taking care of first things first—which is why he always worked with his clients to address their spending habits before moving on to how to invest their money. You simply had to make a habit of spending less than you earned. It sounded simple, but Tom knew that it was anything *but* for most people, especially nowadays with easy credit, online shopping, debit cards, automatic withdrawal, and so on. There were a million ways to spend money without ever having to think about the consequences. But the consequences would come around, whether you thought about them or not. Fortunately, Tom knew how to help his clients overcome these obstacles to financial fitness. Years ago, he developed a coaching service in his practice to help families build the foundation for financial fitness. His service focused on educating people with respect to the real value of implementing a sound budget and spending-management plan. He found that if clients went through this process before developing their long-term financial plan, it made a significant difference in their ability to achieve financial success.

He picked up the phone halfway through the first ring. "This is Tom."

"Hi, Tom. This is Ryan Richardson. I just made an appointment for my wife and me to meet with you. Shirley transferred me to you for an introduction."

"How are you, Ryan?" Tom boomed. "I have to admit, I've heard quite a bit about your family over the years. Shirley is quite a fan of you and the kids. She mentioned that you might be calling sometime after the New Year."

"Yes," Ryan responded. "I think push has finally come to shove for Christine and me. We had a bit of a cash-flow situation right before the holidays and, well, let's just say we had more than one heated conversation about it. I think we're really ready to make a change. We just don't want to live with this hanging over our heads any longer. Of course, I'm sure you hear this all the time these days, especially after the holidays."

Tom smiled. He knew Ryan was making a bold move just making this call. "Ryan, I can tell that you and Christine must have thought a lot about this before you made this call. You've already scheduled an appointment, so it sounds like you are well on your way to making a commitment to managing your finances. So many people make that a resolution but never actually take a proactive step of doing something about it. You're halfway there just by having this conversation and deciding that you may need some assistance. I'd be happy to help put you at ease with your financial situation. I think that once you've decided to make a change in the way you think about money, the next steps will follow naturally."

"Thanks, Tom," Ryan said. "At ease is exactly where we want to be."

■ ■ ■ ■ ■

For their first meeting, Tom requested that Ryan and Christine bring statements and information about each of their consumer debt accounts, car and home equity loans, mortgages, and any other debts they were regularly paying, along with information about their savings and investment account balances. Ryan almost laughed when Tom mentioned savings *and* investment accounts. *He's going to think we are complete failures when he looks at how little we have accumulated over the past ten years,* Ryan thought.

As Ryan and Christine stepped off the elevator into the reception area decorated in muted, warm tones, they waved to Shirley, who was sitting in front of a computer screen at her desk.

Shirley had anticipated their arrival and had coffee waiting for them. She thought they might be a little nervous about meeting with Tom.

"Thanks so much, Shirley. You're the best," Ryan said.

"No problem. I just heard from David," she said. Ryan and Christine had left Chad and Jennie with Shirley's 13-year-old son David, who was very responsible for his age. "He said the kids just had a snack and are doing fine. I'm glad it worked out with him watching Chad and Jennie. It sounds like they are all having a ball."

"Well, I'm glad someone in the family is," Christine said with an ironic smile. "I guess we're just hoping your boss doesn't think we're a couple of idiots when he sees the state of our finances."

Shirley smiled. "You're not the only newcomers to walk in with a bit of anxiety. It's not the easiest thing to do. I should know. You know how hard it was for me to get on top of things after Russell and I split up. But Tom's a good guy, and I think you'll be happy with him and what he has to say."

Ryan looked around. On the lamp table were copies of a number of personal finance magazines. On the wall was a large, framed chart titled "The Success Cycle." Before Ryan could digest the detail on the chart, Tom walked in and greeted them.

"You must be the Richardsons."

"Yes." Ryan rose to shake his outstretched hand. "I'm Ryan, and this is my wife, Christine."

"Hi, how are you?" he said and shook Christine's hand. "Please call me Tom. Ryan," he said, "it's great to put a face to the voice. Nice to see you both." He led them into his office, where he invited them to sit at a small conference table. "Let me start by telling you a little about myself and why I love my work," he began. He explained that he had received a finance degree from the University of Michigan in 1967 and for the past 32 years had been working with clients who, from an income perspective, could be described as middle-class Americans. Typically, his average client began working with him at the age of 35 or 40 and had a household income of less than $100,000.

"We've come for some professional advice," said Ryan, "and it certainly sounds like we fit your profile. We've tried for years to stick to some kind of a budget, but we keep sliding back into our old spending patterns. I guess old habits die hard."

"Let's see if I can help. To begin, I'd like to know something about your financial history. Specifically, tell me about the financial environment you grew up in and your financial history during your marriage."

Ryan began by telling Tom a little bit about his background, where he grew up and went to school, what his parents did, and so on. He had to admit that, if he was really honest about it, his parents were never all that good at managing their money, and that he probably learned some bad habits from them when it came to personal finances. He then discussed the money problems he and Christine had had since getting married, and how they never seemed to get better no matter how much more they made. Christine filled in the blanks as Ryan told their story, and then talked about her own upbringing.

"My parents were always good at saving money and managing their finances," she told Tom, "but it always seemed so much simpler to me when I looked at their situation compared to ours. And not because we have less income–it just seems harder to keep track of everything these days." Tom listened intently and asked a few clarifying questions along the way as Christine described how their predicament had worsened over the past few months, despite the added income.

Half an hour later, Tom said, "I think I have an adequate picture of your present situation. For the next few minutes, let's see if we can put together a statement of your net worth."

Ryan and Christine provided the details, and Tom took out a blank sheet of paper and scratched out the statement. On the top part of the sheet, he listed all of their assets: the market value of their home, cars, furniture and personal property, savings account, checking account, and 401(k) account. Below that, Tom listed all of their debt obligations, including their primary mortgage, home equity loan, car loan, credit card balances, Ryan's student loan, and miscellaneous consumer debt. Tom totaled both columns and then subtracted the debt obligations from the assets. At a quick glance, Ryan and Christine had a present net worth of about $20,000. (See Figure 2.1.)

Ryan and Christine stared at the paper on the table. Considering the nice home they owned, they had assumed they were worth much more. But the numbers told the truth, and they could not hide from it. After 12 years of marriage, they had managed to accumulate only $20,000. Their cash-equivalent assets, including assets from a 401(k) plan and a savings account, totaled less than $7,500.

Not exactly enough to retire on, Ryan thought as he looked nervously at Christine.

"That's not bad," Tom said. "You actually have a positive net worth."

FIGURE 2.1 ■ Richardsons' Net-Worth Statement

Richardsons' Net-worth Statement

ASSETS	
House	$225,000
Savings	$2,300
401k	$5,000
Autos	$17,400
Misc. Personal Property	$15,000
TOTAL ASSETS	$264,700
LIABILITIES	
Mortgage	$206,320
Home Equity Line	$9,875
Auto Loan	$14,750
American Express	$4,855
Visa	$4,350
Student Loan	$3,950
Department Store	$435
TOTAL LIABILITIES	$244,535
NET WORTH	$20,165

Ryan glanced at Tom in surprise.

Tom continued, "Let me share some information that you may find startling." He began to lay out for them some troubling statistics on the state of finances in America. Among other things, he told them that:

- Total consumer debt exceeds $1.8 trillion.
- The average consumer debt per household exceeds $17,000.
- The average credit card debt per household is $6,500.
- The average American has nine credit cards.
- 70 percent of Americans live paycheck to paycheck.

Ryan and Christine were shocked. If the saying "misery loves company" was true, they certainly had plenty of company. Ryan was especially surprised with the amount of debt the average family carried.

Tom looked at them and said, "The lack of personal financial management and the high levels of consumer debt have created a personal financial epidemic in America over the past several years. The number-one asset for Americans has always been equity in their homes. Yet over the past ten years, as interest rates have declined and banks have aggressively pursued the home equity loan market, many consumers have transferred their debt obligations to their homes. Today, the average equity in our homes has actually declined."

"Well, we're guilty," said Ryan. "We thought it was a way to avoid paying high interest rates."

"It can seem that way," replied Tom. "This type of strategy for debt management, while sound by the numbers, is problematic, because families often do not fix the root cause of their debt woes. Home equity loans, in fact, may actually mask the extent of the overspending problems in a family and even put their home at risk."

"I don't think I ever thought of it like that," admitted Ryan.

"What the average family does next," Tom explained, "speaks to the epidemic we are faced with in America. Because they have not addressed the overspending problems, families often go out and repeat the cycle all over again. My experience leads me to believe that the average family actually spends about 10 percent more than they bring in annually, whether they make $50,000 or $500,000 per year . . . "

"Well," joked Christine, "at least we're no worse than average."

"There are millions in your same situation, Christine," Tom agreed, "and many more who are doing far worse. Let's take the example of the average family spending 10 percent more than they earn. If they have an after-tax income of $50,000, they will usually spend closer to $55,000 a year. Over the course of three years, they will likely accumulate about $15,000 in consumer debt, carried primarily in credit card balances and miscellaneous revolving debt accounts. That is the point at which many consumers seek a home equity loan or a refinance of their primary mortgage." Tom looked thoughtfully at Ryan and Christine and added, "Such a step can be deceiving and lead a family to think they are nearly debt-free, since all their credit card balances and revolving debt accounts have been wiped clean."

Christine looked at Ryan and said, "That sounds familiar. We did feel relieved at the time. But now we're right back in the same mess, only worse."

Tom nodded. "It's a common pattern. Your debts aren't really wiped clean, of course. They're just consolidated into one debt account with a lower interest rate: one monthly payment instead of three or four. As I say, it makes sense by the numbers. But it does give a false sense of security and never really addresses the root problem."

"Whew!" Ryan leaned back in his chair. "You've just described our finances to a tee. It's not a pretty picture, is it?"

Tom chuckled, but added seriously, "Ryan, as I mentioned to you in our telephone conversation, just the fact that you and Christine are here shows me that you have a desire to get on a different path. Unfortunately, most people never make it to this point. They just go right on spending and jeopardizing their financial future and the future of their family."

Christine spoke up, "We want to put the brakes on our spending, but everything always seems important at the time. We never intended to live beyond our means—I guess we just figured at some point, we'd be making enough money to get us out of debt."

"It seems that, from what you're saying, Tom, we could have the same problems no matter how much we're making," said Ryan. "We're here because we want to make some changes. We just don't know what changes to make."

"Helping you to refocus is a good place to start," responded Tom. "Recent studies have shown that people earning average incomes who eventually become wealthy have three things in common: First, they live well below their incomes. Second, they believe that financial independence is more important than high social status. And third, they allocate their time and energy efficiently in ways conducive to building wealth."

Ryan and Christine exchanged glances. "Well, we certainly don't qualify on number one," said Christine.

Ryan nodded in agreement. "It's really hard to say no to spending money."

"My personal opinion," Tom added, "is that most people are often unable to really focus on the third, because they never get beyond the first two. To say it differently, it is very difficult to find the time and energy necessary to maximize our earning potential when we are caught in the daily grind of trying to manage debt loads and worrisome financial situations. True financial independence comes when we free ourselves of debt and know that we have the resources necessary to meet all of our financial obligations, including retirement."

"That's what we want," Ryan agreed.

"I am convinced that, statistically, it is very unlikely that we can earn our way to financial independence," said Tom. "Individuals who succeed must first successfully tackle the number-one financial issue facing American families: spending management."

"I agree with you," said Ryan, "but finding an answer to that problem is not all that easy. Christine and I are both educated people. Our intentions have always been to stay out of debt and grow our savings for the future. But somehow, with all the complexities of life, we have failed miserably. And if your numbers are right, we are not alone."

Tom leaned back in his chair. "You're right, Ryan. It's not that simple, but it's not all that difficult, either, if you apply the right principles and use the right tools. Tell me, what do you do over at Medical One?"

Ryan explained his position and the responsibilities surrounding his job.

"And how do you keep your projects on budget?" Tom asked.

Ryan paused as he remembered his promotion to senior project manager. Medical One had created a very successful process for project management. He began to explain to Tom that when he took over as the senior project manager, the company had sophisticated project-tracking software and a number of other management tools in place. Still, most projects were coming in over budget. Senior management's number-one objective for him was to find a way to manage projects within the budget. Ryan had focused on two areas: first, accurate forecasting, and second, expense management.

Ryan believed that Medical One had the first mastered. And even if it didn't, merely raising the cost forecast would be a competitive disaster, because the company would have to charge more. Obviously, Medical One was not making as much as it should on projects, because the projects were coming in over budget.

He explained that his biggest frustration with expense management was that the company's accounting system was always about one month behind. It was nearly impossible, without keeping complex spreadsheets and spending a lot of time he didn't have, to determine how a particular expense item would impact the overall budget.

Ryan had taken a good look at the tools available to Medical One for planning and tracking project expenses in real time. After studying many products, he found a module that would integrate with Medical One's current accounting system, making it possible to do real-time tracking of all expenses, including labor. This meant as soon as a purchase or expense item was approved, it was logged to the project, which allowed managers to know immediately where they stood financially. Ryan recommended to senior management that Medical One spend the $75,000 necessary to purchase and integrate this new expense planning and tracking system. He had made a solid presentation, and senior management had approved the upgrade.

After rolling out the new system, Ryan and his project managers always knew exactly how much money remained in each budget, and how each new expense would impact the overall budget. With few exceptions, the project management team had delivered projects on or under budget. Senior management was pleased. The $75,000 investment was going to pay for itself many times over.

As he concluded, Ryan broke into a smile. He suspected that he had just stumbled onto one of the key issues he and Christine faced with managing their personal spending.

Tom spoke. "Ryan and Christine, are you familiar with the Success Cycle?"

Ryan recalled the chart in the reception area. "No," he said, "but I think I saw it hanging outside your office."

"That's right," Tom said. "The Success Cycle describes the process used by many companies to successfully plan and execute a project to completion. The steps include planning, tracking, comparing, and adjusting. Ryan, I believe this is the process you have just described in your work for Medical One."

Ryan nodded.

"The component you were missing was real-time tracking, making it impossible for a manager to make appropriate comparisons to his budget or to make needed adjustments to keep the project on track."

Ryan was following him and nodded, "Yeah, that's right."

Tom pulled a document from a file folder and handed it to Ryan and Christine. On it was a copy of the chart Ryan had seen in the re-

FIGURE 2.2 ■ Success Cycle

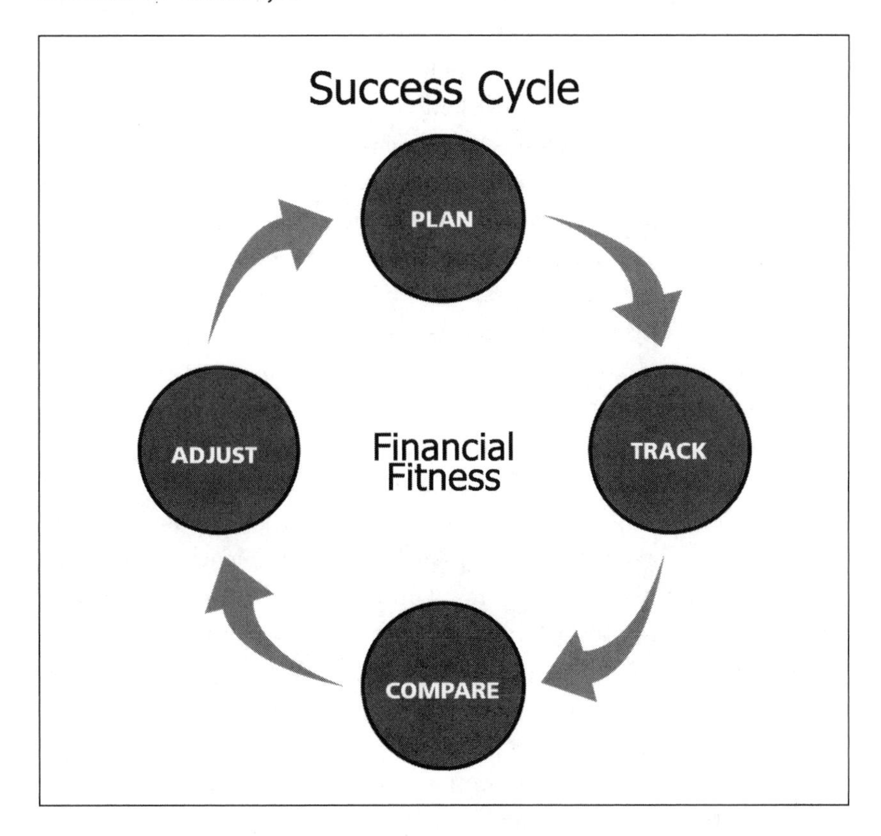

ception area. In the center were the words financial fitness. Around this were four steps, with arrows leading from one to the next. Starting at the top, the steps were labeled PLAN, TRACK, COMPARE, and ADJUST. (See Figure 2.2.)

"Personal financial management in today's world is much like that of a company," explained Tom. "Without planning, it is impossible to create a benchmark against which to measure success. Tracking is a vital component, and I don't mean haphazard recordkeeping like most people do, but tracking every single expenditure."

"Track every purchase!" exclaimed Ryan. "How would we even begin to do that? That was the problem at work until we found the tracking software–there was just no realistic way to track all of our expenses in real time."

"That would be a real hassle and sounds almost impossible," added Christine. "Tracking expenditures at Ryan's company is one thing, but in real life it seems so complex. So much of what I end up buying only costs a few dollars. Some things I charge, some I pay cash for, and for others I write checks. I know it'd end up driving me crazy."

"It's important, though," explained Tom. "Just like the system you implemented at Medical One, once a couple begins to successfully track each expenditure, they can compare the results to their original plan. It is impossible to plan perfectly the first time, and therefore adjustments will be necessary. As couples continue this process, they become very good at managing spending and maximizing savings and investments. They also can avoid the consumer debt trap."

"That all sounds good in theory," Christine said, "but the realities of day-to-day living make following that cycle difficult."

"You're right," Tom said.

Suddenly Ryan leaned forward and said, "We found a tool for our company; it would be nice if we could find a tool that would be able to track our personal expenses on a daily basis and summarize our spending status for us. Accurately planning and tracking in real time is nearly impossible. I've just never found anything that can track as I spend."

Tom sat back and thoughtfully said, "You two have just identified the two major problems most people face with finances: first, understanding the realities of spending in today's environment, and second, finding the tools necessary to implement the success cycle."

"Our problem exactly," agreed Ryan.

"Let me tackle the realities of spending in today's environment first. In my opinion, there are a number of root problems we face today. Each of these problems has an impact on our spending psychology. Here is a list." Tom pulled a sheet of paper from a file folder on the table. On it was a list of several root causes of poor spending choices:

1. Loss of a psychological tie to real money
2. Explosion of ways to spend money
3. Inability to compare expense to income in real time
4. Lack of training
5. Advertising-driven consumption
6. Easy access to consumer credit

"Let's take a few minutes and discuss each of these," Tom said. "First is a loss of a psychological tie to real money. In the past, people purchased items mainly with cash. When the money was gone, it was gone. Today, individuals use a lot of plastic and revolving consumer accounts. Actual tests have shown that on average, individuals will spend 10 to 12 percent more for the same items and services with plastic than they will with cash. We are losing the psychological tie that comes with making a cash transaction. It's just too easy to spend 'invisible' money today."

"I know!" exclaimed Christine. "It is so convenient to pull out a credit card. I've always been so good at managing the checkbook, but when it comes to credit cards, I've just never gotten past the idea of them being 'free money.' I tend to look at the credit limit as if it's our own money, instead of money we will potentially have to pay back. It's just too easy to forget how real that negative balance will become."

"You are only doing what many people do," Tom said. "The second issue, which is related to the first, is an explosion of ways to spend money. When I was just getting started in this business, there really were only a few ways the average person could spend money–mainly by using cash or by writing checks. Today, there are numerous methods for spending money, including credit cards, debit cards, direct payment, online bill pay, and revolving credit accounts, as well as cash and checks. On top of this, most families, in addition to carrying a number of credit cards, have multiple checking and savings accounts–often with more than one bank. As a result, tracking spending has become even more difficult than before. It's hard enough to track one person's spending in this complex environment. When you add two or more spenders to the average family, it becomes nearly impossible."

"Yes," agreed Ryan. "Even when we tried to plan our spending, we never knew for sure if the other one had already spent the money or how much was left. It's frustrating."

"It's a big problem, all right. This added complexity leads to the next problem, an inability to compare expense to income in real time."

"Ryan," Tom said, "you talked about the tracking software program purchased by Medical One. This software allowed you to see the impact of every spending decision on a specific area of the project budget and on the project overall."

"That's right," Ryan added.

"Well," Tom continued, "the complexities of our modern world have made it very difficult to compare our daily and monthly spending to the income we have coming in. For most people, it is nearly impossible to understand if they can really afford a particular purchase. Without being able to evaluate each purchase on a daily basis as it relates to our weekly and monthly income, it is very difficult to make informed decisions.

Christine sighed and said, “I know exactly what you mean.”

“Now, let’s look at the fourth issue leading to poor spending choices—lack of training. When was the last time the two of you had any formal training in the area of personal financial management?” Tom asked.

They both shook their heads, and Christine said, “I don’t think I ever received training in that area, even in college.”

“That’s just it,” Tom said. “As a society, we do a very poor job of providing even basic personal financial management training. Given the complexity of managing finances in today’s world, it is no wonder people have such a difficult time.

“The fifth factor is advertising. It is hard to avoid spending when you are bombarded with thousands of marketing messages every day. They come at us from radios, televisions, outdoor advertising, retail outlets, and public transportation, just to name a few. Making purchases as a result of advertising is known as ‘advertising-driven consumption.’ The fact is,” Tom continued, “American companies are very good at marketing. It is very difficult to appropriately combat these messages and place them within our own proper need-versus-want category. Advertisers do a great job of making us believe we need everything.”

“I keep thinking I am resistant to advertising, but I’m probably being influenced in ways I don’t realize,” admitted Christine.

“We all are,” Tom agreed. “And, to make it even harder, companies provide easy access to consumer credit. When was the last time you received a credit card offer in the mail?”

Christine, who normally opened the mail, responded, “Just yesterday. In fact, I’ll bet we get several offers each week.”

“That’s right,” Tom answered. “And when did you get your first credit card?”

Ryan thought for a minute, then said, “I think it was my sophomore year in college.”

“And how difficult was it to get that card, and what was your credit limit?” Tom asked.

"Well, let's see," Ryan said. "It took a while to get it, and I think the credit limit was around $1,000."

Tom chuckled. "That's where we have come in just the past 15 years. Today, we have high school sophomores with credit card debt problems. Fifteen years ago, banks would have scoffed at the idea of extending credit to a high school student. Consumer credit has gotten completely out of hand, and consumers are all too eager to use the full amount of what is extended to them."

Christine nodded. "I know all about *that.* When you put it all in perspective like this, it is easy to see how spending and consumer debt have gotten so far out of control."

"Yes," said Tom. "Without a clear plan that implements the principles and the right tools necessary to execute that plan, it is almost impossible for the average American to achieve personal financial objectives."

Ryan and Christine shifted in their chairs, trying to anticipate where Tom was going with all this.

Tom continued, "I wanted to talk to you about some of these root causes, because it will make clear the plan of action I'm going to suggest."

"Well," said Ryan, as he looked over the sheets of paper in front of him, "I certainly feel like I have a better understanding of what we've been doing wrong."

"I agree," said Christine. "And I also feel a little bit better in knowing that we're not the only ones with this problem."

"I think I can speak for both of us," Ryan said, "when I say we'd like to know which path we should take."

■ APPLIED PRINCIPLE 6
Take a candid assessment by preparing a net-worth statement.

When you join a fitness club for the purpose of losing weight or becoming physically fit, you will usually participate in an assessment of your level of physical fitness. A fitness coach will determine your current weight, measurements, body-fat ratio, and resting heart rate to define the best starting point for your fitness program. As you move forward with the program, your coach will take ongoing measurements and review the progress made.

This initial statement of physical health is very important. Without knowing where you are, it is difficult to understand where you need to go. This information becomes much more black and white when it is put into writing.

Before you can move forward in a meaningful way, you need to candidly assess your current financial position. Your initial personal net-worth statement is much the same as the physical fitness assessment. When Ryan and Christine met with Tom, he requested that they bring the information to the meeting that would allow them to create this initial net-worth statement. The three of them carefully reviewed and compared the items the Richardsons had acquired that had some commercial value (assets) with the debts they had amassed over the years (liabilities). Many financial professionals view your net-worth statement as the measurement of your personal wealth. A positive net worth indicates that the monetary value of your assets is greater than the total of all your liabilities. Negative net worth indicates you owe more in debt than the total monetary value of what you own.

In their bestselling book, *The Millionaire Next Door,* authors Thomas J. Stanley and William D. Danko unveiled a comprehensive study of finances in America. As an introduction to this profound study, the authors wrote:

> Why are so many people interested in what we have to say? Because we have discovered who the wealthy really are and who they are not. And, most important, we have determined how ordinary people can become wealthy. What is so profound about these discoveries? Just this: Most people have it all wrong about wealth in America. Wealth is not the same as income. If

you make a good income each year and spend it all, you are not getting wealthier. You are just living high. Wealth is what you accumulate, not what you spend.

Many people with average to high incomes have relatively low net worth. The financial challenges facing most Americans are not dependent on the amount they earn but on how they manage what they earn.

According to Stanley and Danko, nearly one-half of all personal wealth in the United States is owned by only 3.5 percent of the households. Their 1996 study suggested that more than 25 million households in the United States had an annual income greater than $50,000, with more than 7 million households earning more than $100,000. Despite having relatively high incomes, most of these people had low net worth. Their study pointed out that the typical household in America has a net worth of less than $15,000, not including the equity in the home. If you were to take away the value of motor vehicles, furniture, and other personal items, often the household net worth fell to nearly zero. According to the same study, most households have no financial assets, such as investments and long-term savings.

To begin reversing these trends in your own life, you need to candidly assess your financial health by completing a personal net-worth statement. Completing this statement is not very difficult and can be done in a short amount of time by following three simple steps.

STEP 1: Make a list of your assets and their corresponding value.

The first list to compile is your cash-equivalent assets. This includes the balance in your checking accounts, savings accounts, 401(k) accounts, IRA accounts, the cash value of life insurance policies, and the current market value of stocks, bonds, or other marketable securities. You may also include in this list money owed to you, as long as you have a reasonable likelihood of collecting the outstanding balance. (See Figure 2.3.)

The second list to compile is your real estate holdings. This includes the market value of your home and any other property you own. To approximate the value of the real estate you own, you can check with the

FIGURE 2.3 ■ Cash-Equivalent Assets

Personal Net-worth Statement

Assets			
	Cash-equivalent		
		Checking Account	$1,000
		Savings Account	$2,500
		401k Accounts	$7,500
		Misc. Stocks	$4,000
	Total Cash-equivalent		$15,000

Realtor who sold you the house or a Realtor who works in your neighborhood. They can quickly complete a competitive market analysis for you. And, in most cases, they are quite willing to help. You also may have a recent appraisal report on hand. This report would give you an approximate value as well. You need to exercise some caution if your recent appraisal was completed as part of a home equity loan or a refinance of your existing mortgage, as these appraisals can often be 2 percent to 10 percent high. (See Figure 2.4.)

FIGURE 2.4 ■ Real Estate Assets

Personal Net-worth Statement

Assets			
	Real Estate		
		Primary Residence	$235,000
	Total Real Estate		$235,000

The final list of assets would be an itemization of personal property. This would include the current value of vehicles, furniture, and higher-priced personal property like recreation vehicles, jewelry, collectibles, and, perhaps, electronic equipment. To determine the current value of your vehicles, visit http://www.bluebook.com and provide the required information. To approximate the value of other personal property, sub-

FIGURE 2.5 ■ Other Assets

Personal Net-worth Statement

Assets		
Other		
	Auto 1	$5,000
	Auto 2	$12,500
	Furniture	$8,000
	Jewelry	$4,000
	Misc.	$2,500
Total Other		$32,000

tract 25 percent of the purchase price for each year you have owned the item. Jewelry and collectibles generally hold their value much better than furniture and other personal property. Using the purchase price of these items is a safe approximation of their value. If they were received as a gift, you may need to have a professional assess their value. (See Figure 2.5.)

STEP 2: Complete a list of all debt obligations (liabilities).

In this step, list all of your debt obligations. Start with the current amount you owe on your house, home equity loans, and debt consolidation loans. Then, list the amount you owe on vehicle loans. Finally, list the balance owed to all consumer debt accounts, including personal loans, student loans, charge accounts, credit card accounts, and any other type of consumer debt. You should be able to find the current balance for each of your debts by checking your most recent statement or by checking for the balance online. (See Figure 2.6.)

STEP 3: Calculate your net worth.

To finalize the calculation of your net worth, total the value of all assets listed. Then total the value of all liabilities listed. Once you have completed these calculations, subtract the total value of your liabilities

FIGURE 2.6 ■ Liabilities

Personal Net-worth Statement

Liabilities		
	Mortgage	$199,000
	Home Equity Loan	$24,000
	Auto 1 Loan	$2,500
	Auto 2 Loan	$9,750
	Credit Card 1	$6,900
	Credit Card 2	$4,350
	Student Loan	$2,800
	Furniture Store	$4,500
	Department Store	$750
Total Liabilities		$254,550

from the total value of your assets. The resulting number is an approximation of your current net worth. (See Figure 2.7.)

At this stage, it is critical that you be completely honest with yourself on the value of your assets and make sure you have created a comprehensive list of all debts. As was the case for Ryan and Christine, the first time you see this number in black and white, you may be startled or disappointed. The idea here is not to cast you into deep despair, but to see where you are today and to provide a benchmark to measure against in the future. Place a date on the statement you have just created and be prepared to create a new statement every three to six months. You will be amazed at how quickly you can make meaningful progress when you have become committed to following the path to financial fitness.

FIGURE 2.7 ■ Net-Worth Calculation

Personal Net-worth Statement

Assets		
Cash-equivalent		
Checking Account	$1,000	
Savings Account	$2,500	
401k Accounts	$7,500	
Misc. Stocks	$4,000	
Total Cash-equivalent	$15,000	
Real Estate		
Primary Residence	$235,000	
Total Real Estate	$235,000	
Other		
Auto 1	$5,000	
Auto 2	$12,500	
Furniture	$8,000	
Jewelry	$4,000	
Misc.	$2,500	
Total Other	$32,000	
TOTAL ASSETS	$282, 000	$282,000
Liabilities		
Mortgage	$199,000	
Home Equity Loan	$24,000	
Auto 1 Loan	$2,500	
Auto 2 Loan	$9,750	
Credit Card 1	$6,900	
Credit Card 2	$4,350	
Student Loan	$2,800	
Furniture Store	$4,500	
Department Store	$750	
TOTAL LIABILITIES	$254, 550	$254,550
NET-WORTH		$27,450

■ APPLIED PRINCIPLE 7

Spend less than you make.

Stanley and Danko also found that the path to substantial net worth was similar for many wealthy people in America. Most had modest incomes and had accumulated their wealth over a number of years. This approach to financial fitness suggests a prudent attitude toward money. While most people can point to one or two examples of someone who received a significant windfall of money, the likelihood of this event is very slim. Many times, those who have earned substantial incomes have the same level of poor financial health as those who earn much less. Those who have amassed great wealth seemed to understand a critical point with respect to money: A person will be much more successful in achieving true, long-term financial fitness if they focus first on living within their means. The true secret lies in the way we choose to spend our money rather than in the way we choose to earn our money. While there are many ways to earn money, there really is only one way to accumulate wealth–spend less than you make! Tom understood this principle and had used it over the years to help many clients reorient their financial thinking and spending habits. With this financial approach deeply rooted, you will be better prepared to successfully manage more money as you have opportunities to increase your income in the future.

The same philosophy holds true for a company. If a company is losing money, management has two choices: increase revenues or cut costs. If they are not successful at achieving one of these two, the company will soon be forced to close its doors. Have you ever heard someone say, "If we only had more sales, we would be profitable"? Or conversely, "If I only made more money, I wouldn't be forced to go into debt"? Truly successful companies find ways to spend less, thus ensuring profitability at any level of sales. Sometimes, this means making difficult decisions regarding cutting costs, including reducing staff. As sales increase, a well-managed company will continue to monitor spending to ensure that it falls within acceptable limits. By following the principle of spending less than they take in, the management of a company will ensure the long-term viability of the enterprise.

The process is the same for individuals. Each of us has a personal company to manage. We have sales in the form of salary or income. And we have costs in the form of house payments, transportation costs, and general living expenses. If we want to create a financially healthy enterprise, we must make choices to spend less than we make. The flip side to this approach leads to an increasing debt load and a complete lack of resources to meet the needs of future spending requirements. Statistically, it is very unlikely you will be able to achieve financial fitness by simply earning more money. You must first apply the principle of spending less than you make. As soon as Ryan and Christine clearly understood and accepted this principle, they began to make significant progress toward becoming financially fit.

■ APPLIED PRINCIPLE 8

Implement the Success Cycle.

Once you have adopted the principle of spending less than you make, you are on your way to winning the mental financial fitness battle. When you make up your mind to become physically fit, you need to develop a plan or adopt a system, including eating right and participating in an appropriate level of exercise. Usually, this will assist you in focusing your efforts toward successful achievement. The same is true for achieving financial fitness. After you have determined that you will take the steps necessary to become financially fit, you need to incorporate a system into your personal financial life.

Tom introduced Ryan and Christine to a very important concept called the "Success Cycle." Simply put, the Success Cycle is a system that can be adopted and routinely followed to ensure continued improvement and long-term financial fitness. This system includes four steps: planning, tracking, comparing, and adjusting. (See Figure 2.8.)

While the system seems relatively simple, when these steps are followed continuously, the results can be extraordinary. Successful companies everywhere incorporate this system into their monthly, quarterly, and annual management systems and processes. General Electric, one of the world's most successful and consistent companies, has perfected the Success Cycle. Successful project managers, contractors, and process management professionals all follow this cycle. What's more, this cycle can be applied to a very small project spanning a few weeks, or to the construction of a multi-billion-dollar industrial plant spanning a number of years. In either case, successful execution requires that each of the steps in the Success Cycle be taken; steps cannot be shortened or eliminated. Americans often like to find the quick fix or the silver bullet. What we need to realize is that victory comes through the steady and persistent application of proven principles.

Some years ago, Frank Burge, a noted publisher, told a story regarding management styles in an article in *Electronic Business* magazine (7 October 1991). His story related a conversation between him and Alex d'Arbeloff, chairman of Teredyne. Apparently, d'Arbeloff had been trying to figure out why the Japanese were so successful. Was it because they're just smarter than us? No, he thought, they're smart, but no smarter than us. Is it because they work harder? Again, they work hard,

FIGURE 2.8 ■ Success Cycle

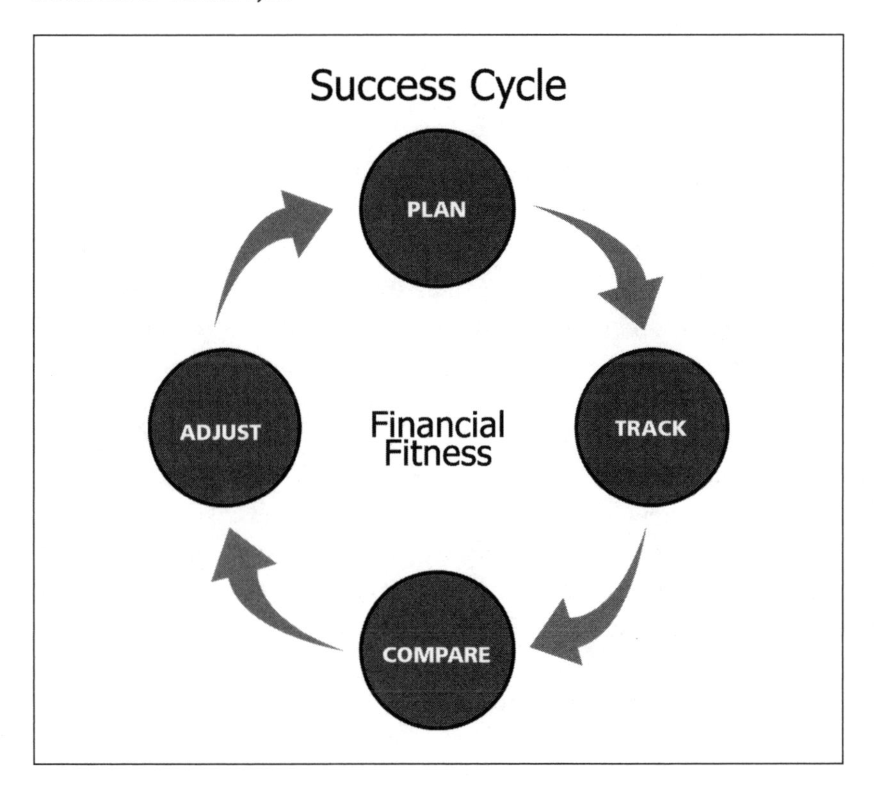

but American workers are some of the most productive, hardest-working people in the world. That can't be it, either.

Then it dawned on him. He realized that most Americans tended to operate their businesses by managing events. When something goes wrong, we fix it. We manage to put out fires very well—what d'Arbeloff refers to as "fire-hose management"—but what we fail to do is improve the processes that could prevent fires in the first place. Our motto usually is, "If it ain't broke, don't fix it."

The Japanese, on the other hand, run their businesses by managing processes. They make sure that they understand the process inside and out, and then they focus on making continuous improvements in the process—not necessarily monumental changes, but small, incremental adjustments. That takes patience. In effect, their motto is, "If it ain't broke, make it just a little bit better."

If you run your company by managing events (putting out fires), your company is never going to improve. At the end of five years, you'll have the same company you had when you started. But if your competitor is managing its processes and focusing on continuous quality improvement over those same five years, it is going to become a much more efficient, productive, and successful company.

After Burge finished his presentation, a man in the audience made this observation: "Frank, the difference is the Japanese are farmers. They sow the seed. They water it. They let the sun nourish it. And then they harvest it. Farming takes patience. You just can't rush the process. Americans aren't farmers; Americans are hunters. When they want dinner, they go out and shoot something. Bang! It's done. 'Forget patience. I'm hungry.' 'Bang!'" When the gentleman finished his comments, everyone in the audience was laughing–they recognized the truth in what he was saying.

Consistent implementation of the Success Cycle will force us to become more patient–to be more like farmers and less like hunters. This will ensure our long-term financial success. Tom understood it was important for Ryan and Christine to implement the continuous improvement process naturally facilitated by following the Success Cycle. If you wish to correctly implement the four steps in the Success Cycle, you need to clearly understand each one.

STEP 1: Create a plan.

Without a plan, you will find it difficult, if not impossible, to find your way through the maze of personal financial complexity. Few of us would consider taking a trip to a new location without first consulting a map and planning the best travel route. So it is with financial fitness. After you have created a net-worth statement, you need to determine the direction you will take next. This includes carefully planning the way you will spend your money on a monthly basis. Planning is a process that successful companies follow meticulously. Often, these plans include detailed monthly, quarterly, and annual information regarding sales, expenses, profit, and cash management.

Your monthly personal financial plan should include both a summary of the income you expect to receive during the month and a detailed plan for spending during the month. As with all types of planning, until you have reduced the plan to writing, either on paper or on the computer, it is not really a plan but only a wish. This book will teach you how to create an effective monthly plan.

STEP 2: Track every transaction.

Once you have completed a monthly plan, you need to begin tracking your progress. Companies in America spend billions annually tracking every transaction, including sales, expenses, and cash receipts. Imagine trying to successfully manage a company without using and applying accounting principles. Some try, but largely they either have low levels of success or fail. This should not be surprising. Why then do so many try to achieve personal financial success without tracking their income and expenses?

Companies don't choose which transactions to track—they track every transaction. *The only way to get the complete value from tracking is to track every transaction.* If you want to become financially fit, you must be prepared to carefully follow this principle. Tracking every transaction can seem overwhelming at first, but with the right tools, this can be very simple. In this book, you will learn about some of these tools and how to utilize them successfully.

STEP 3: Compare your actual performance to your plan.

A written plan does little good if you don't take the next step of comparing your actual results against your plan. Again, well-managed companies utilize the comparison process on an ongoing basis. Budgetary managers in these companies receive monthly, quarterly, and annual comparison reports. These reports highlight the areas for review.

With physical fitness, a coach will test your performance at regular intervals and compare the new information with past results. This will allow you and your coach to understand the areas in which you have improved and those areas that may require some changes. It is the same with financial fitness. The step of comparing your actual results with your plan is a crucial one. This includes looking at both income and expenses. Planning and tracking do you very little good if you are unwilling to take time to compare your results on at least a monthly basis. As you make this comparison, you will immediately understand how and where to make necessary adjustments.

STEP 4: Make adjustments.

It is nearly impossible to create a perfect plan the first time around. Great planning is a process that includes both time and experience. As you plan, track, and compare, you will be able to see clearly which areas need to be adjusted. These adjustments may include adding spending in some areas and reducing it in others. The entire process does you little good if at the end of your review you are unwilling to make necessary adjustments. Good managers take the information provided from comparison reports and then make appropriate adjustments. These include changes that impact both sales and expenses, ultimately enhancing the overall profitability of the enterprise. Each time you complete the cycle by making necessary adjustments, your plan will become more accurate. You will be surprised and amazed at the adjustments you can make over time.

■ ■ ■ ■ ■

Following the Success Cycle will allow you to incorporate processes followed by successful companies and project managers. You will be prepared to immediately implement the principles of the Success Cycle when you are finished reading this book. As Ryan and Christine will soon learn, doing this will assist you in reaching your financial fitness objectives.

Chapter Three ■

Choosing a New Path

Tom had in mind the best solution for Ryan and Christine as soon as he understood their situation. They needed a budgeting system that would give them control over how they spent and that would offer them a preview of the consequences of their purchasing decisions. Like anything that required a shift in thinking, it would take some time to develop, but would pay off, so to speak, in the end.

"Are you familiar with the traditional envelope method of cash and spending management?" he asked them.

Christine smiled and said, "You mean the process of stuffing your cash into different envelopes? One for gas, one for clothing, one for vacation, one for food, right?"

"That's right," Tom said.

Christine continued, "My grandmother did that for all the years I knew her. She absolutely swore by it! But I never really understood how it worked. How could mere paper envelopes help someone save money?"

"Well," Tom said, "there is a reason your grandmother, and literally thousands like her, used this system in the past. With this system, purchases were primarily made with cash. After taking a paycheck to the bank and cashing it, an individual would take the cash and literally divide, or allocate, it to spending accounts created with labeled envelopes.

FIGURE 3.1 ■ Traditional Envelope Budgeting System

There were usually two types of envelopes: those for monthly purchases, like food, clothing, utilities, and housing, and those for purchases that took place periodically, like vacations, property taxes, gifts, insurance payments, and so on. For monthly purchases, an individual would determine the amount of required monthly spending, and after receiving a paycheck, would fund, or place, the required amount of cash into these envelopes. (See Figure 3.1.) For periodic purchases, a person would determine the annual required spending and then divide this amount by 12. Then each month, this amount was placed into those envelopes.

"Whenever cash was needed to purchase groceries, a person would take the envelope labeled FOOD to the grocery store. With cash in hand, two very important pieces of information were available: first, how much money was left to spend, and second, how long it would be before there was cash to put into that envelope again."

"So they could never overspend the grocery budget," commented Christine.

"That's right," Tom said. "But in today's high-tech, cashless society, we have lost complete track of this information. That old envelope system made it possible for individuals to easily plan, track, compare, and adjust their spending—all four components of the Success Cycle."

Ryan leaned forward. "That's fascinating," he said. "The envelope system provided individuals with the same type of information that the new accounting system at Medical One provides for our project managers. The only problem with using the envelope system today is the need to have cash on hand. That really isn't practical in today's world."

"So true. Who pays their mortgage with cash these days? No one. That's just not practical anymore. The amazing advantages of the envelope system have not disappeared, however. The traditional envelope system worked fine if you used only cash. Most people today, however, are unwilling to give up the flexibility of their debit cards and checks—and when you combine cashless spending with the old system, you lose the ability to track in real time. But there are several ways to implement the envelope system in our modern era. I'll tell you more about these in our next meeting."

He paused and waited for the reaction of his newest clients. Just as he thought they would be, they were interested but cautious.

"So where do we go from here?" Ryan asked.

"What I really want you to accomplish this week is to set up your spending plan. First, you'll need to figure out your total net monthly income—all the money you actually have to spend. Next, you'll want to get a good picture of all of the different places your money goes. That's why you'll need to set up spending accounts—essentially, your envelopes—that take into account every category of spending that you have. This can take a little time to complete. To help you think about what those are, you should create two main categories of expenses: monthly and periodic. And divide each of those categories into two more: required and discretionary. Monthly required expenses are things like your mortgage and car payment—expenses that must be paid each month; monthly discretionary expenses include things like, clothing, entertainment, and groceries—things that are always there but are variable and over which you can exert some control. Periodic required expenses would include property taxes, annual auto registration, and homeowners insurance; periodic discretionary expenses would be things such as vacations, gifts, and home maintenance.

"Once you've calculated your income and identified your spending categories, you're ready for the third step—figuring out how much money you're spending, on average, in each category. You should spend some time looking at the information you have on hand, and use that information to determine how much you've been spending in each category every month. Don't worry if you're not able to find all of the specific data, because we'll be making adjustments as you start tracking your spending. The idea is to get a general sense of your spending. You'll use this information to estimate how much you're spending in each category every month, compare that to your monthly income, and then—the fourth step—decide how you will start reducing your spending. That's how you create your spending plan, which leads to understanding how to start managing your money."

Tom suddenly looked very serious. "Ryan and Christine," he said, "my job as a certified financial planner is to help you invest your excess cash in ways that will assist you in reaching your financial objectives. To get to that point, I am also interested in working with you to create a financial plan that will make that happen. Over the years, I have prepared many sophisticated financial plans for clients. These clients have paid thousands of dollars for these plans. Unfortunately," Tom continued, "because a large number of these clients have not been able to spend within their income and save money, they have abandoned these plans. If clients are unable to generate excess cash over time, there is little or nothing I can do to help them achieve long-term objectives."

"First, we have to manage our spending," said Christine.

Again, Tom agreed. "Once you've done that, then you'll learn to pay down debt and start saving. Let's meet again next week, and then once a month for the next three months. In our next meeting, I'll show you a tool that you can use to implement the envelope system. But we're getting ahead of ourselves here. For now, set up your spending plan. This requires some effort, but I know it will make a difference in your finances and in how you are looking to plan the future. Is this something that you believe is worth the time?"

Christine grabbed her husband's hand. "I know it is."

■ ■ ■ ■ ■

A sea of fourth graders bolted up out of their desks en masse as the end-of-day bell rang out through the hallways of Christine's school.

"Now, kids, don't forget your reading assignment for tomorrow," Christine said loudly, above the din of nine-year-old chatter and horseplay. "We'll be going through the first half of chapter six in your red books in the morning."

For once, Christine was as excited as her students were that the school day was over. She and Ryan had set aside this evening to go through their finances with a fine-tooth comb. And since she would be getting home earlier, Christine agreed to set up a basic spreadsheet to help them create their spending plan. She stuffed a few papers into her bag and headed out the door.

The key for Ryan and Christine tonight was to budget their income by creating envelope spending accounts. Tom had prepared them for this step with some counsel. "When you create your envelope spending accounts," he had told them, "you will be creating your monthly spending plan. Your total spending must fit within your defined monthly net income." He suggested that the two of them spend some time in advance trying to define all of their areas of spending and the amount they had typically spent per month in each area. They had started doing this a few nights before but were going to nail down those details this evening.

As Christine drove home in the car, she started cataloguing some of the expenditures in her head. She and Ryan were both excited to be taking this step, but she was afraid that they'd find it impossible to spend less on a regular basis. *What if there is no room in our budget to squeeze?* Christine thought. *On the other hand,* she thought, *at least if we go through with this, we'll know exactly what the situation is. And that's got to be a plus, no matter what.*

Christine opened the front door of their house and let out a deep breath. Silence. For once, the house was quiet. She'd gotten her friend Susan to take the kids this afternoon. Susan and Rob Goldman had been friends of Ryan and Christine's since college. Rob had been Ryan's roommate during his freshman year, and they'd been close ever since. Susan and Rob had two kids—Megan, their 14-year-old who had just entered high school, and Danny, who was 8. Chad and Jennie were probably having a blast with Megan and Danny by now. Megan was great with Chad and Jennie, and such a good student. Christine frequently told Megan what a great teacher she would make, and secretly hoped that she might someday follow in her footsteps.

Their office at home had become another play area for the kids—toys were strewn about the floor and on the desk. Chad loved to play games on the computer, and even Jennie was using it now. Christine thought back to the first time she started using a computer. It was at the

University of Florida–they had a small computer lab next to her dorm where she typed up her papers for class. When she learned how to type in junior high, it was on a typewriter. *My kids don't even know what that is,* she thought, *and Chad is already a better touch typist than I ever was.*

She cleaned up the office as best she could, turned on the computer, and began to set up a spreadsheet to categorize their expenses on one side and their income on the other. She and Ryan had begun putting together a list on paper of all the categories of expenses they had–mortgage, car loan, credit cards, student loan, home equity loan, taxes, insurance, utilities, groceries, clothes, dining out, entertainment (movies, shows, playing golf), personal care, vacations, gasoline, car maintenance, home maintenance, day care, babysitters, music lessons for Chad, swimming lessons for Jennie, allowances, Christmas gifts, and pocket money. The sheer variety of spending categories was intimidating. *No wonder it was all so hard to keep track of,* she thought.

Categories of income, on the other hand, were relatively simple to track–Christine's job at the elementary school and Ryan's job at Medical One, plus bonuses.

She entered the spending and income categories into the spreadsheet and left spaces to fill in the numbers. At the bottom of the screen was a space labeled TOTAL. That would be the one to tell them just how much they were overspending each month.

Next, Christine gathered together all of their credit card, loan, and bank statements, along with any other utility statements and bills from the past year. They would need to go over these to confirm the numbers they had come up with earlier in the week for how much they were spending every month in each category. By now, it was time to pick up the kids from Susan and Rob's house. Ryan would be getting home just about the time she got back.

■ ■ ■ ■ ■

Ryan sat at his desk reviewing Medical One's latest project reports. It was still early in the month, but so far things seemed to be on track. As he pondered a few of the details on one of his larger projects, the phone rang. It was Christine.

"Hi honey, it's me," she said. "I'm on my way to pick up Chad and Jennie. I was just calling to let you know that I set up the spreadsheet for us on the computer."

"That's great, Christine. Sounds like you've been busy. I appreciate your doing that."

"I actually kind of enjoyed it," she said. "It's a little tiring, gathering everything together like that and trying to cover every category of spending. But it's exhilarating when you think about what we'll know about our situation when we're done."

"That's true," Ryan said. "And we'll be able to use it to help us stay on track from here on out."

"I'm looking forward to working together on it," said Christine. "I'll see you at home."

"I should be home in a half hour, depending on traffic. See you then."

Ryan hung up the phone and found himself smiling as he packed up his briefcase. For the first time in many months, there was reason for hope. And frankly, their taking productive steps together to solve the problem was creating some good feelings between them–something he welcomed.

As Ryan rounded the corner and pulled into the driveway, he saw Christine and the children sitting on the porch waiting for him. Chad and Jennie ran to Ryan's door almost as soon as he parked the car. They both spoke excitedly about their day at school.

"Hey, slow down you two," Ryan said, laughing. "Let's take it one at a time. You go first, Jennie."

His daughter broke into excited chatter about her day in kindergarten. Soon, Chad chimed in. As a third grader, he loved math and science.

"Hey, Dad," Chad asked confidently, "what's 10 times 100?"

Ryan pretended to think for a minute. "Well Chad, I'm struggling with that one. What is it?"

Chad quickly replied, "It's 1,000, Dad. Why didn't you know that?"

Ryan laughed. "It's been a long time since I studied math, Chad, and I'm a little rusty. So you're going to have to keep helping me."

After dinner, Ryan helped Chad with his homework while Jennie colored and Christine cleaned up the kitchen. Then they started the bedtime routine, which included reading stories and tucking the children into bed.

Finally, Ryan and Christine were sitting together at the computer. Ryan looked over the long list of spending categories on the spreadsheet and practically gasped.

"Wow," he said. "No wonder we can never keep track of all of this stuff by ourselves. Look at all of the ways we have to spend our money."

"That's funny. That's exactly what I thought when I looked at this list," said Christine. "OK, now let's figure out our total monthly income."

"Yes," Ryan said, "it'll be nice to start with something positive."

Ryan opened up the file of pay stubs he had gotten out the night before and started doing some math on the calculator. "Starting from my gross salary at Medical One of $64,000," he said, "my annual take-home pay after taxes, Social Security, health insurance, and my 401(k) comes down to $46,092.28. If I divide by 12, I get a monthly income of $3,841.02."

Over the past several years, Ryan's bonus had grown proportionately with his salary, except for the rare quarter when objectives had not been met. Because they could not be certain of the amount they would receive, he looked at the bonuses paid out over the past two years and entered the average. "If I average out my bonuses from the last eight quarters," he said, "I get an average quarterly bonus of $895.85, which, divided by three, equals an additional monthly income of $298.62. Add that to my monthly salary, and the total is $4,139.64."

"Whew!" said Christine. "I thought you told Chad your math skills were rusty."

"OK, let's do yours now," said Ryan. Christine figured her monthly after-tax income to be $2,096.67. "So our total combined net monthly income is $6,236.31." Christine looked at the number and said, "My gosh, we should be able to live on that! Why are we always scraping to get by?"

"I'm not really sure, but I think that's what we are about to find out."

Next, Ryan and Christine started work on the spending categories—the envelope spending accounts they were about to create. They each had estimated monthly budgets for each category. With the credit card and other bills and statements spread out on the desk in front of them, they began to look at the hard evidence. Most of what they estimated was accurate. But there were a number of surprises.

"This is good news," said Christine. "Our monthly utilities come out to be less than what I remembered they were."

"Yeah," said Ryan, "but the bad news is we're spending more on gasoline than I thought. And if these MasterCard bills are right, we're definitely spending more on clothes than you thought."

In some categories, it was tough to face the truth of how much they were spending each month. But they started assigning real numbers to the numerous spending categories Christine had entered into the spreadsheet earlier. As Tom had suggested, they then divided the categories, or envelopes, into four kinds of expenses: monthly required and discretionary, and periodic required and discretionary. Ryan was studying the dwindling amount of money left for discretionary spending. "Cursor down the screen," he said to Christine. "It looks like you still have a lot of categories of spending here."

"These show where the rest of our money goes," she said. "Clothing, allowances, eating out, entertainment, activities for Chad and Jennie, vacations, Christmas gifts, and pocket money."

Ryan looked at Christine. "Wouldn't it be nice to have all the money we needed for Christmas set aside in advance next year?"

Christine grimaced and nodded. The memory of the credit card experience at the checkout line was still fresh in her mind.

Christine began entering the remaining numbers and soon noticed they were getting to a negative number. "We're overspending, Ryan. Look."

"Keep going. Let's see by how much."

Christine entered the last of the amounts on the spreadsheet. They looked at the final total. There it was. They were spending nearly $600 a month more than they were bringing in.

Christine looked at Ryan and sighed, "Well, where do we go from here? We've included everything, and we're falling behind by over $7,000 a year."

Ryan looked at Christine and said, "Well, when we got to this point at work, we had two choices: increase prices or track spending so we could manage within our budget." Christine nodded, and Ryan continued, "I don't think our situation is all that different. We can hope for an increase in income, or we can work to manage within the resources we have."

Christine knew Ryan was right. "Based on the numbers we came up with here," she said, "we'll have to trim $587.46 from our monthly budget."

They spent the next 20 minutes looking at each spending envelope and made decisions about what they had to cut back on. After a while, nothing was sacred. Christine watched in amazement as Ryan reduced his golf and recreational spending account. Ryan was taken aback when Christine cut down her clothing and personal care allowance.

"We might be cutting a little too deep in some areas," Christine warned. "One of the things that worries me is our ability to stay within the envelope budgets when it comes to putting this into practice."

"That's OK. We'll talk to Tom about it next week. The important thing is that we have it prepared."

Finally, the plan was balanced. While Ryan printed out the spreadsheet from the computer, he looked over their budget on screen. "Well," he said, "we're not saving much, but at least now we can start to pay down some of our debts."

"You're right," Christine acknowledged. "If we stick to this plan, we will have stopped the overspending. And who knows, maybe we can find other places to save as we go along."

Ryan nodded his agreement. "You know, this has been revealing. I'm anxious to see if we can make it work. Remember what Tom said? Something about the absolute feeling of empowerment that comes from having the money set aside for the things we need, when we need them.

"I like knowing exactly what I can spend. I don't have to feel guilty every time I go shopping–you know, wondering if I buy something today if we'll still have enough to pay the bills tomorrow."

Ryan sat back and reached for Christine's hand. They had just completed the first step in the process–developing a balanced spending plan that would allow them to live within their means. The plan would initially allow them to begin eliminating consumer debt, something both of them wanted to accomplish as soon as they could. And eventually, they would have money to save or invest.

"Thanks for doing this with me," Ryan said as he leaned forward to shut down the computer. "I'm really excited to give this a try."

"I'll do everything I can, as well. Now we'll always know exactly where we stand."

"I think we've taken a real step forward with this . . . "

"Shush." Christine put her arms around Ryan and gave him a kiss.

■ ■ ■ ■ ■

"How's my favorite couple?" asked Tom, as he gave Ryan and Christine a wink and ushered them into his office.

It had been three days since Ryan and Christine had spent the evening working out their new budget. After completing the work of identifying their envelope spending accounts, discovering by how much they were overspending, and figuring out a workable, balanced spending plan, they were eager to move on to the next step. Tom had promised to show them a way that would help them implement–and stick to–their new budget. They sat down across from Tom at the table.

"Well," said Tom, "did you find my assignment useful?"

Ryan and Christine shared a smile. "We found the homework to be well worth it," said Ryan.

"Yes," Christine agreed, "we feel like we have a much better understanding of the problem and what we can do about it."

"Right," said Ryan. "Now we're just anxious to find out how we can use what we've learned to keep ourselves on track."

"Good," said Tom, as he leaned forward and uncapped his pen. "Last week, I described the traditional envelope budgeting system to you. The system is very simple, and it's what you used as the basis for creating your spending plan. Each category in your spreadsheet is, in essence, a virtual envelope. There's nothing more to the old-style envelope system than what I shared with you last week–you literally have an envelope filled with a set amount of cash for each spending category. When the envelope runs out, that's it. You either wait until next month, or take money out of one of the other envelopes, thus reducing the amount you can spend in that category.

"It's a foolproof system," continued Tom, "as long as you only use cash. When I started out more than 30 years ago, that was a reasonable assumption. Except for paying bills, most people still used cash for almost all of their purchases. However, as we discussed, the proliferation of debit cards and other forms of payment have made cash-based envelopes workable in theory but unrealistic in practice for most people. It just isn't practical to use cash the way we used to. Fortunately, there are other solutions available for those who don't wish to live a cash-only lifestyle."

Ryan and Christine leaned forward in their chairs as Tom continued.

"The good news," said Tom, "is that there is now a way to keep track of all of your purchases with your computer. Much like the tracking software you identified at Medical One, Ryan, there are tools I can show you that will do much the same thing, except they will be tailored for your personal spending. By accessing your financial institutions, you can track, in real time, all of the purchases you make. And with the right software, you can assign transactions to the appropriate 'envelopes.' So, you can still use your envelope budgeting system without having to go back in time to the 1950s when everyone used cash.

"Of course," Tom continued, "you can still use actual cash envelopes for certain things, if you want. The idea is to make sure that you're keeping track of your spending as you go along, day by day. You also can use a paper ledger, or spreadsheet, system, if you choose. Since I know you're both pretty capable on the computer, a computer-based system might be right for you."

Ryan looked at Christine. "I think we'd both jump at the chance to be able to use a tool that could assist us in tracking our spending in relation to our various spending categories in real time. It sounds like the ideal solution."

"Terrific," replied Tom. "I'll work with you to set up your envelope budgeting system. Once you feel comfortable with it, I would like to challenge you to use it for the next 12 weeks. If you use the system as planned, I am confident it will change your life. Following your successful use of the system for 12 weeks, we will begin developing a long-term financial plan. Are you up to the challenge?"

"Absolutely," said Ryan.

"I would like to meet with you once a month to review your progress. At our next meeting, we'll talk about some debt-reduction methods that can be used with your envelope system."

"That's great," said Christine. "How do we get started?"

■ APPLIED PRINCIPLE 9

Learn the secret of envelope budgeting.

Isn't it amazing how often we learn about simple principles that, when applied, have the ability to impact our lives in profound ways? Such is the case with the traditional envelope method of personal financial management. Many have heard of or are familiar with someone who has used this simple system for spending management. The envelope system has worked exceptionally well for many people in the past. These people understood the basics of the system and how to use it, but many could not articulate the principles behind the system that allowed them to be successful. Tom clearly understood the principles associated with the envelope system and was eager to introduce these to Ryan and Christine.

The envelope system as it was used with cash is very simple. In the days before the proliferation of credit cards, debit cards, and other forms of cashless spending, many couples were very dedicated to this system and used it effectively for years. Initially, a couple would sit down together and determine how much cash they would receive each month. This available cash represented the net amount of all of their paychecks for the month. Then, they determined where they would be spending money. Their areas of spending included things that they would purchase and pay for each and every month, and things that they would spend money on only periodically. After completing their list, they took out a stack of envelopes and labeled one for each area of spending. Their next task was to determine the amount of money required for each envelope every month. For the areas of periodic spending, they calculated the amount they would spend each year, and then they divided this amount by 12. This represented their monthly spending plan.

When they received a paycheck, they would go to the bank and cash the check. Then they would sit together at the kitchen table and divide the cash into different envelopes based on their defined spending plan. When they paid for goods or services, they would simply spend from the specified envelope. The envelope became a self-policing spending account. Couples always knew how much money they had left to spend and how long it needed to last. (See Figure 3.2.)

The envelope system automatically encapsulates four principles that are keys to financial success. They reveal the secrets of how you can achieve financial fitness utilizing the envelope system.

FIGURE 3.2 ■ Traditional Envelope Budgeting System

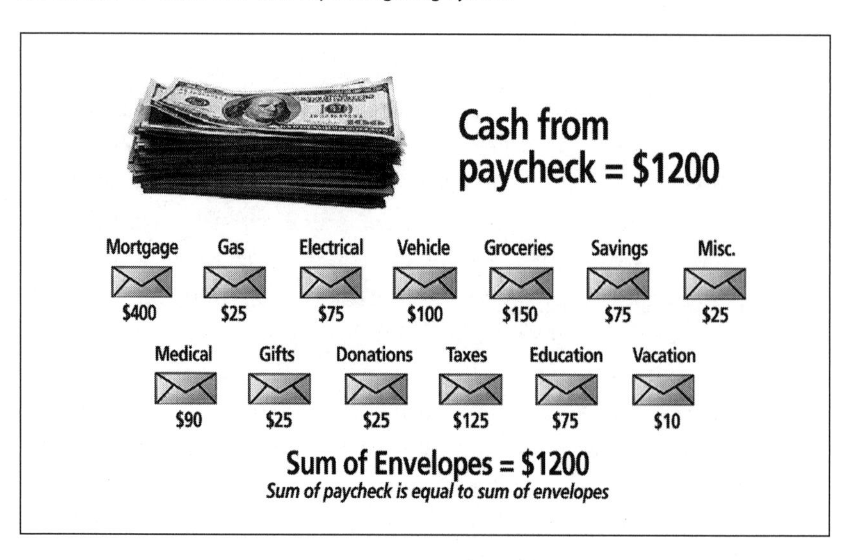

FIRST: Set money aside in advance.

When you commit yourself to the use of the envelope system, you become dedicated to living within your means. One of the primary reasons for this is that the envelope system requires you to set aside money in advance for each of the spending requirements you have, including monthly required and discretionary and periodic required and discretionary expenses. As discussed earlier, many people in America live paycheck to paycheck. The envelope system helps eliminate this problem, because the funding for spending comes from available cash resources that are allocated to spending before the spending takes place. After following this system for just a few months, you can quickly get to the point where you have enough money set aside at the beginning of the month to meet all of that month's spending requirements.

One of the significant problems people face today is not understanding how future spending requirements will impact their monthly cash flow. Have you ever had an annual insurance payment surprise you? Other periodic spending requirements include vacations, property tax payments, holiday spending, gifts, auto registration fees, auto maintenance fees, house maintenance fees, furniture and appliance replacement costs, and so on. As you think about it, there are many things that can catch you off guard if you don't plan ahead. These types of expenses were constantly creating problems for Ryan and Christine. Much of their consumer debt was directly associated with being unprepared for periodic spending requirements.

Most people manage spending by their checking or savings account balance at the bank. Unfortunately, this account balance does not prepare you for the periodic spending needs that will arise in the coming months. It also does not alert you to the spending your partner is planning over the next few days or weeks. So you make independent decisions about how much you think you can spend without really understanding the big picture. This is a very dangerous approach and leads to problems, including bounced checks, frustration, and, ultimately, more debt. Most of the overspending in families can be traced to an inability to incorporate periodic spending requirements into their current cash resources and spending practices. A great example of this is the amount of credit card debt that is created during the holidays or on vacations each year as a result of not having money set aside in advance. Many justify this spending by telling themselves that they will pay the credit card balance next month. This rarely happens, because next month's spending requirements are already based on 100 percent of the cash resources for that month.

The envelope system addresses this problem of periodic spending requirements by allowing you to set aside money in advance of periodic spending needs. For example, if you were going to spend $2,400 on Christmas each year, you would be setting aside $200 each month. To state this another way, if you want to spend $2,400 each year for Christmas, you need to spend $200 less on other things each month.

Perhaps your parents or grandparents used an envelope budgeting system. Imagine how they felt each December when they prepared to purchase gifts for Christmas and the Christmas envelope was full! Imagine how you will feel when you want to take a vacation and know that the money is already set aside in advance. Or imagine how nice it will feel to know that you have money set aside to replace the tires on your car the next time it's required. The envelope system holds the secret to setting aside money in advance.

SECOND: Spend from how much is left.

One of the significant secrets to not overspending is to know daily how much you have left to spend in any area of defined spending. While this seems very simple and even obvious, consider how often you make purchases without knowing how much you can really spend before your spending outstrips your available resources—or how many times you buy something without knowing how it will negatively impact your ability to meet other spending requirements. The unplanned gift purchase had a significant impact on the resources Ryan and Christine had for other spending requirements. When people used the traditional envelope system to make purchases—to buy clothes, for example—they would take the clothing envelope with them. They knew immediately how much they had left to spend and how long it had to last before they funded the envelope again. This information was invaluable in assisting them to make sound spending decisions. If you choose to spend less than you make, then spending from what's left becomes very simple. If there is not enough in the envelope to complete the purchase being considered, the purchase is delayed or another purchase decision is made. Without knowing how much is left, you can only hope that the purchase decision you are making will not negatively impact other areas of your financial life. Unfortunately, you will not know this until it is too late. Knowing in advance how much is left to spend is the secret to making smart spending decisions every day.

THIRD: When you run out, you must make a choice.

We all want to be fully empowered to make choices. Often, this is one of the justifications we make for spending money. "It's my money, I've earned it, and I have the right to decide how to spend it! If I want to purchase that coat, I will, period." The problem with this thinking is that it often takes choices away later on: because you purchased that coat, you may not be able to purchase the birthday gift you wanted for your daughter.

The envelope system does not eliminate the ability to make personal choices; it provides information so you can make more informed decisions. With the envelope system, it is quite possible to run out of money before you fund the envelope the next time. If this happens, you have three options: (1) put off the purchase until you fund the envelope the next time, (2) purchase something less expensive, or (3) purchase the item and transfer money from another envelope to cover the cost. All three choices will still allow you to live within your means. With the third option, you can determine at the point of purchase which other area of spending you would like to impact. For example, if you wanted to purchase the coat and didn't have enough money in the clothing envelope to cover the cost, you could transfer money from your groceries envelope to cover the cost. If you made this decision, you would do it with the knowledge that you would not be able to spend as much on food this month. There's nothing wrong with having made this choice. Perhaps you know that your grocery needs were less this month than in the past, or perhaps you did not spend all the money in your grocery envelope last month and you have extra. Whatever your thinking, you have to be able to make a purchase decision and understand exactly what impact it will have in other areas of your financial life. Making a purchase choice is great as long as you do it on an informed basis. The envelope system holds the secret to truly empowered purchase decision making.

FOURTH: At the end of the period, what's left is savings.

One of the key principles to securing financial fitness is to save something first. In addition to setting aside a specified amount for savings each month, the envelope system allows you to save the balance remaining in many envelopes at the end of each period. For example, if you have some money left in your groceries envelope at the end of the month, you could take that money and apply it to savings, since you would be funding the envelope with enough money next month to take care of your needs for that period. Many of your discretionary spending envelopes would qualify for this review at the end of each period. Discretionary spending envelopes are envelopes covering areas of spending that are not tied to fixed or required expenses. Based on the spending decisions you make in these areas, you may often have money left over at the end of each period. Examples of discretionary spending envelopes include clothing, groceries, eating out, entertainment, and so on. By adding the amount left in each of these envelopes to your defined savings, you can significantly increase the amount you apply to savings, debt repayment, or long-term investments. The envelope system holds the secret to increased savings.

■ ■ ■ ■ ■

While people in our grandparents' day used cash to successfully implement the envelope system, it is more difficult today. Many purchases can still be made conveniently with cash; however, we often pay for goods and services using checks, debit cards, credit cards, online bill pay, and even automatic withdrawals from our bank accounts. For some, the cash-based envelopes may represent the best approach for ensuring financial management success. For others, cash may simply not be a feasible alternative. The envelope principles outlined above are not dependent on the implementation tool used. As a result, you can successfully incorporate the envelope process using one of four basic approaches: (1) cash, (2) a paper ledger or computer spreadsheet, (3) a computer-based envelope system, or (4) a combination of these. Appendix B on page 155 provides more insight into these alternatives and discusses the successful implementation of each.

■ APPLIED PRINCIPLE 10

Create a spending plan.

Regardless of the approach to the envelope system you choose, the starting point is always the same. You must first develop a spending plan. This can be done successfully by following these four steps.

STEP 1: Define your net monthly income.

Before you can develop a detailed spending plan, you must first understand the amount of resources you have to work with. In other words, what is your net income? As most of your bills are paid on a monthly basis, you need to calculate the amount of net income you have each month. For fixed income sources, this can usually be calculated very easily. With variable income sources, it can be a little tricky.

Let's start with fixed income sources. Most of you receive a paycheck that represents your net pay. This net amount is what's left after taxes and employee benefits like insurance have been subtracted from your gross pay. Next, you need to look at how often you receive your paycheck. If you receive one paycheck each month, your monthly income is simply the net amount of that check. If you receive a paycheck twice each month, your net monthly income is the net amount of your check multiplied by two. If you receive a paycheck every other week, you need to multiply the amount of your paycheck by 26 (the number of paychecks you receive in a year) and then divide this amount by 12. Finally, if you receive a paycheck once each week, you need to multiply the amount of your paycheck by 52 and then divide this number by 12. (This monthly net income calculation is shown in Figure 3.3.)

Make sure you calculate the monthly net income for each of your fixed income sources. If you receive a paycheck every two weeks, you will have two months of the year when you receive three paychecks. As a result, you may want to be cautious in your approach to the net monthly income calculation. Because this extra money is received only once every six months, you may prefer to determine your net monthly income on the basis of two paychecks each month. Then, for the months where you receive a third paycheck, determine in advance to apply this to a periodic spending envelope, extra savings, or additional debt reduction.

FIGURE 3.3 ■ Net Income Calculation

Net Income Calculation

Frequency of Paycheck	Net Amount of Paycheck	Number of Paychecks per Year	Annual Net Income	Monthly Net Income
Every Week	$1,000	52	$52,000	$4,333.33
Every other Week	$1,000	26	$26,000	$2,166.67
Twice each Month	$1,000	24	$24,000	$2,000.00
Once each Month	$1,000	12	$12,000	$1,000.00
Once each Quarter	$1,000	4	$4,000	$333.33
Once each Year	$1,000	1	$1,000	$83.33

* To calculate 'Annual Net Income,' multiply the 'Net Amount of Paycheck' by the 'Number of Paychecks.'
To calculate 'Monthly Net Income,' divide the 'Annual Net Income' by 12.

One other area of caution with fixed incomes is overtime. If you are paid hourly and you receive overtime pay, you can use one of two approaches: (1) if you only receive overtime pay occasionally, you can just treat it as upside pay and not include it in your net monthly income calculation, and then allocate it as you receive overtime; or (2) you can take a look at the overtime pay you have received for the past several paychecks and use the average amount to calculate what your net monthly pay will be.

Once you have made these calculations, write the name of each fixed income source on a sheet of paper together with the corresponding amount of net pay. (See the Richardsons' fixed net income in Figure 3.4.)

Let's move now to calculating your net income from variable income sources. Variable income sources include commissions, bonuses, and other sources of income that may vary in amount and frequency. Because of these variations, you need to be cautious with respect to your approach to calculating the amount of net monthly income.

If you receive a commission payment every month, you can use either the smallest monthly commission received over the past several months, or you can calculate the average amount received each month. The same is true for bonuses.

Sometimes commissions and bonuses are paid quarterly, semiannually, or even annually. In this case, you can calculate the amount you con-

FIGURE 3.4 ■ Richardsons' Fixed Net Income

Richardsons' Fixed Net Income

Income Source	Net Income	Pay Periods per Year	Annual Net Income	Monthly Net Income
Medical One	$1,772.78	26	$46,092.28	$3,841.02
Washington Elementary	$1,048.34	24	$25,160.04	$2,096.67

servatively expect to receive annually and divide this amount by 12. You need to be cautious here, because you will be developing a spending plan based on your net monthly income, and if this variable income represents a large percentage of your total net monthly income, you may find yourself overspending for large portions of the year.

Financially fit people whose sole source of income is variable find ways to set money aside when they receive it, so they can use it appropriately until they receive their next paycheck. Generally, these people determine their total monthly spending requirements and then use this number as their calculation of the amount of income they need to allocate to monthly spending. This way, they do not spend more than they have allotted, and they will have the appropriate amount of money set aside for future spending requirements. If a large portion of your total income is variable, refer to Appendix C for additional insight into using the envelope system with variable income. (See how the Richardsons handled variable net income in Figure 3.5.)

Once you have made these calculations, write the name of each variable income source on a sheet of paper together with the corresponding amount of net monthly pay.

After you have completed a list of both fixed and variable income sources, calculate the total of all income sources. This number represents your net monthly income. (See Figure 3.6 for an example.)

FIGURE 3.5 ■ Richardsons' Variable Net Income

Richardsons' Variable Net Income

Medical One Quarterly Bonus	
Check 1	$1,099.90
Check 2	$918.89
Check 3	$892.65
Check 4	$890.85
Check 5	$840.73
Check 6	$852.89
Check 7	$829.94
Check 8	$840.95
Total	**$7166.80**
Average	**$7166.80/8= $895.85**

FIGURE 3.6 ■ Richardsons' Total Net Income

Richardsons' Total Net Income

Income Source	Net Income	Pay Periods per Year	Annual Net Income	Monthly Net Income
Medical One	$1,772.78	26	$46,092.28	$3,841.02
Washington Elementary	$1,048.34	24	$25,160.04	$2,096.67
Medical One Bonus	$895.85	4	$3,583.40	$298.62
Total			**$74,835.84**	**$6,236.31**

STEP 2: Define areas of spending (spending accounts).

Once you have defined your net monthly income, you are ready to define your areas of required spending. For purposes of consistency, let's call these spending accounts. Remember from our earlier discussion that there are two types of spending accounts: monthly and periodic. Monthly spending accounts are areas of spending that have spending activity each month. Periodic spending accounts are areas of spending that have spending activity only periodically—for example, quarterly or even annually.

Let's first deal with the monthly spending accounts. Monthly spending accounts can be either required or discretionary. Monthly required accounts include things like car payments, the minimum or planned payments for credit cards, mortgage payments, etc. Because saving something first is a very important principle to adopt, you should also set aside a fixed amount each month for savings. Monthly discretionary accounts include things like groceries, eating out, clothing, entertainment, allowances, etc. On a sheet of paper write down each of the monthly spending accounts that are applicable to you. Separate these into required and discretionary. (See the Richardsons' example in Figure 3.7.)

Second, let's address periodic spending accounts. As with monthly accounts, these also can be split into required and discretionary spending. Periodic required accounts include things like property taxes, periodic insurance payments, annual auto registration fees, etc. Periodic discretionary accounts include things like gifts, vacations, house maintenance, holiday spending, etc. On your sheet of paper, write down each of the periodic spending accounts that are applicable to you. Separate these into required and discretionary. (See Figure 3.8.)

STEP 3: Define the amount of monthly spending for each spending account.

After you have created a complete list of your spending accounts, the next step is to determine the amount of monthly spending for each account. Starting with the list of monthly spending accounts, determine an amount that represents your historical spending for this account. To do this, you may have to look at past statements or receipts. For some

FIGURE 3.7 ■ Richardsons' Monthly Spending Accounts

Richardsons' Monthly Spending Accounts

Monthly Spending Accounts	
Required Expenses	**Discretionary Expenses**
Mortgage	Auto Fuel
Home Equity Loan	Babysitter
Auto Loan	Clothing
Master Card	Entertainment
Visa	Eating Out
Student Loan	Groceries
Savings	Haircuts
Department Store	Spending- Ryan
Music Lessons	Spending- Christine
Fitness Club	Personal Items
School Lunch	Supplies
Auto Insurance	Phone- House
Cable	Phone- Mobile
Power	Books & Magazines
Natural Gas	
House Security	
Water, Sewer, & Garbage	
Day Care	

FIGURE 3.8 ■ Richardsons' Periodic Spending Accounts

Richardsons' Periodic Spending Accounts

Periodic Spending Accounts	
Required Expenses	**Discretionary Expenses**
Auto Registration	Dental Deductible
Property Tax	Doctor Visits Deductible
Homeowner's Insurance	Birthday Gifts
Life Insurance	Holiday Gifts
	Other Gifts
	Auto Maintenance
	House Maintenance
	Vacation
	Donations

FIGURE 3.9 ■ Richardsons' Allocations for Monthly Spending Accounts

Richardsons' Allocations for Monthly Spending Accounts

Monthly Spending Accounts			
Required Expenses	**Monthly Allocation**	**Discretionary Expenses**	**Monthly Allocation**
Mortgage	$1,422	Auto Fuel	$250
Home Equity Loan	$142	Babysitter	$50
Auto Loan	$517	Clothing	$250
Master Card	$75	Entertainment	$150
Visa	$95	Eating Out	$175
Student Loan	$142	Groceries	$425
Savings	$300	Haircuts	$50
Department Store	$75	Spending- Ryan	$100
Music Lessons	$60	Spending- Christine	$100
Fitness Club	$30	Personal Items	$63
School Lunch	$20	Supplies	$20
Auto Insurance	$140	Phone- House	$100
Cable	$55	Phone- Mobile	$120
Power	$150	Books & Magazines	$20
Natural Gas	$60	**TOTAL DISCRETIONARY**	**$1,873**
House Security	$23		
Water, Sewer, & Garbage	$50		
Day Care	$500		
TOTAL REQUIRED	**$3,856**		

accounts, determining this number may be very difficult. If this is the case, try to make a reasonable guess. Remember, after you have created your plan, you will begin tracking all expenses. After the first month, you will be able to make appropriate adjustments.

On your sheet of paper, write the amount you have determined next to each account name. (See Figure 3.9.)

Next, calculate monthly spending requirements for your periodic accounts. The first step is to calculate the amount you will spend in each of these accounts on an annual basis. Write this number next to each periodic spending account on your list. After you have completed this for each account, calculate the amount of monthly spending by dividing the annual amount by 12. Write this number next to the annual amount. (See Figure 3.10.)

After you have completed this total, calculate the total monthly spending. You may also wish to calculate subtotals for your monthly re-

FIGURE 3.10 ■ Richardsons' Allocations for Periodic Spending Accounts

Richardsons' Allocations for Periodic Spending Accounts

Periodic Spending Accounts					
Required Expenses	**Annual Spending**	**Monthly Allocation**	**Discretionary Expenses**	**Annual Spending**	**Monthly Allocation**
Auto Registration	$360	$30	Dental Deductible	$300	$25
Property Tax	$1,980	$165	Doctor Visits Deductible	$720	$60
Homeowner's Insurance	$900	$75	Birthday Gifts	$420	$35
Life Insurance	$600	$50	Holiday Gifts	$1,200	$100
TOTAL REQUIRED	**$3,840**	**$320**	Other Gifts	$180	$15
			Auto Maintenance	$1,380	$115
			House Maintenance	$900	$75
			Vacation	$2,700	$225
			Donations	$1,500	$125
			TOTAL DISCRETIONARY	**$9,300**	**$775**

quired, monthly discretionary, periodic required, and periodic discretionary accounts.

STEP 4: Balance your monthly spending plan.

Now that you have determined your total monthly net income and your total monthly spending, you are prepared to balance your spending plan. A balanced monthly spending plan means that your monthly spending requirements are less than or equal to your total monthly net income.

Begin by calculating the amount you have left after you have satisfied all of your monthly spending requirements. This number is calculated by subtracting your total monthly spending from your total monthly net income. Don't be shocked when you see this number for the first time. Remember, most people in America are spending about 10 percent more than they bring in each month. You may recall this was the case for Ryan and Christine. If you are one of the fortunate few who are spending within your monthly net income, you have a few choices. It is important that you allocate all remaining income to a spending account. Income that is not allocated may be spent in ways that are haphazard and unplanned. To address this possibility, you should allocate the remaining balance to one of your spending accounts, such as savings, or increase the amount you are planning for debt repayment or investments.

Most of us will need to find ways to reduce the amount of monthly spending, so that total monthly spending is equal to total net monthly income. The first spending accounts to review are your discretionary accounts, both monthly and periodic. Review the list you have created and look for areas where you believe you can make downward adjustments to your initial spending amounts. Keep track of the adjustments you are making and subtract these adjustments from the total amount of overspending. Remember, the goal is to live within your means. If you really want to change your financial life, you may need to make some sacrifices. Long-term financial fitness requires dedication to this one principle: Spend less than you make. Thousands of people are making this choice every day, and so can you. As was finally the case with Ryan and Christine, no discretionary spending account should be sacred. If you make these decisions together with your partner, you will be much more successful.

If you still have reductions to make after you have completed a review of your discretionary spending accounts, you will need to begin reviewing your required expenses. Adjustments to these accounts are more difficult, as they usually require more significant changes. Carefully review each required spending account and determine those that can be adjusted. Sometimes you can negotiate reductions in your insurance expenses, or refinance existing debt and qualify for a lower interest rate, thus reducing your monthly payment. You may need to speak to some creditors and negotiate a lower payment until you have eliminated some debt and can increase the amount you are paying. In more extreme cases, you may need to sell some of your assets to reduce your initial debt load. This may mean getting by with one car, selling recreational vehicles, or even downsizing your home. These are difficult choices, but if you are truly committed to becoming financially fit, you may need to make some of these adjustments. When you move forward with these adjustments to ensure a balanced monthly spending plan, you will immediately feel the sense of relief that comes from knowing you are able to live within your means. If you master this principle today, tomorrow you will be able to achieve a level of financial fitness that few others enjoy. After a few short months, you will begin to reap the significant benefits of making these choices.

Once you have created your balanced monthly plan, you will have successfully completed the first step on the Success Cycle. (See Figure 3.11.)

FIGURE 3.11 ■ Richardsons' Balanced Monthly Spending Plan

Richardsons' Balanced Monthly Spending Plan

Monthly Spending Accounts

Required Expenses	Monthly Allocation	Adjusted Allocation	Discretionary Expenses	Monthly Allocation	Adjusted Allocation
Mortgage	$1,422	$1,422	Auto Fuel	-25 ~~$250~~	*$225*
Home Equity Loan	$142	$142	Babysitter	-20 ~~$50~~	*$30*
Auto Loan	$517	$517	Clothing	-75 ~~$250~~	*$175*
Master Card	$75	$75	Entertainment	-55 ~~$150~~	*$95*
Visa	$95	$95	Eating Out	-100 ~~$175~~	*$75*
Student Loan	$142	$142	Groceries	-25 ~~$425~~	*$400*
Savings	$300	$300	Haircuts	-15 ~~$50~~	*$35*
Department Store	$75	$75	Spending- Ryan	-50 ~~$100~~	*$50*
Music Lessons	$60	$60	Spending- Christine	-50 ~~$100~~	*$50*
Fitness Club	$30	$30	Personal Items	-13 ~~$63~~	*$50*
School Lunch	$20	$20	Supplies	-10 ~~$20~~	*$10*
Auto Insurance	$140	$140	Phone- House	-25 ~~$100~~	*$75*
Cable	-20 ~~$55~~	*$35*	Phone- Mobile	-20 ~~$120~~	*$100*
Power	$150	$150	Books & Magazines	-10 ~~$20~~	*$10*
Natural Gas	$60	$60			
House Security	$23	$23			
Water, Sewer, & Garbage	$50	$50			
Day Care	$500	$500			
REQUIRED TOTAL (a)	-20 ~~**$3,856**~~	***$3,836***	**TOTAL DISCRETIONARY (b)**	-493 ~~**$1,873**~~	***$1,380***

Periodic Spending Accounts

Required Expenses	Monthly Allocation	Adjusted Allocation	Discretionary Expenses	Monthly Allocation	Adjusted Allocation
Auto Registration	$30	$30	Dental Deductible	$25	$25
Property Tax	$165	$165	Doctor Visits Deductible	$60	$60
Homeowner's Insurance	$75	$75	Birthday Gifts	$35	$35
Life Insurance	$50	$50	Holiday Gifts	-25 ~~$100~~	*$75*
			Other Gifts	$15	$15
			Auto Maintenance	$115	$115
			House Maintenance	$75	$75
			Vacation	-50 ~~$225~~	*$175*
			Donations	$125	$125
REQUIRED TOTAL (d)	**$320**	**$320**	**TOTAL DISCRETIONARY (e)**	-75 ~~**$775**~~	**$700**

Balanced Spending Plan Summary

	Monthly Allocation	Adjusted Allocation
Net Monthly Income	**$6,236**	**$6,236**
Monthly Fixed Spending (a)	$3,856	$3,836
Monthly Discretionary Spending (b)	$1,873	$1,380
Periodic Fixed Spending (d)	$320	$320
Periodic Discretionary Spending (e)	$775	$700
Total Monthly Allocations	**$6,824**	**$6,236**
Balance *	**($588)**	**$0**

*Net Monthly Income Less Total Monthly Allocations

Balanced!

Chapter Four

Discovering Financial Fitness

Christine and her friend Susan rode up front, with Chad, Jennie, and Susan's youngest, Danny, in the back seat, as they drove to the zoo on Saturday morning. After several minutes of talking about the kids and school, Susan asked, "So how's the 12-week challenge?"

Christine had told Susan how she and Ryan were trying out a new budgeting system. Christine laughed. "You know, it's the strangest thing. This one little thing is making a huge difference for Ryan and me. It's hard to explain, but for the first time in our marriage, I feel like we are on exactly the same page financially. It's made it much easier to talk about money, and much more natural to be conscious of how we're spending. It may be a bit early to tell, but I'm very optimistic."

"Good," said Susan. "I'll be interested to know if you still feel that way in 12 weeks."

They soon arrived at the zoo and headed toward the entrance. Once inside, they asked the kids where they wanted to go first. Jennie wanted to see the ducks, whereas all Chad and Danny cared about were the gorillas and the lions. After spending a couple of hours winding around the paths that took them from aquatic birds to primates to jungle cats, they walked over to the concession stand.

"Mommy, look!" said Jennie excitedly. "A duck hat! Can I have one?"

"I know it's cute, sweetie, but . . . "

"Please, Mommy."

"Well, let's see if we can buy that today," responded Christine. She pulled out her handheld personal organizer and looked at her envelope spending accounts. "It says here that we have some money in our 'Jennie' envelope, but that was to buy you a new pair of shoes this afternoon." Christine looked at her daughter. "So, do you want the duck hat today and the shoes next month? Or do you want to skip the hat and go ahead and shop for shoes like we planned?"

Jennie thought it over, and finally said, "I guess I want my new shoes."

"OK. How about we buy some seeds and feed the ducks?"

"Yes!" Jennie clapped her hands and ran toward the pond, dragging Christine with her.

After touring the zoo, Christine and Susan treated the kids to lunch at a family restaurant that was one of their favorites. While the boys and Jennie took off to check out the gift shop, Susan and Christine had a chance to talk over dessert.

"So, how did you do that at the zoo?" asked Susan.

"How did I do what?" asked Christine.

"You know," Susan said. "Jennie was whining for some duck hat, and you whipped out your organizer and said, 'Well, what'll it be, Jennie, the hat or the shoes?' I mean, how does your organizer know how much money you've got to spend on duck hats? And how did you get Jennie to take it so calmly?"

"Well, Susan," Christine said, "with our new system, we divide our income into a number of spending accounts. Then, every day when we track our transactions, we know how much money is left in all of our accounts." Susan nodded, impressed. "And as far as Jennie . . . well, it doesn't always work that way. But I've found now that I can tell the kids exactly why I can't afford something, and what I *can* afford, and they're much more likely to accept it and move on than when I used to just say 'no'."

"I wish I could get Danny to be a little more accepting," said Susan. "I have a lot of trouble saying 'no' to him when he really wants something. It probably doesn't help that I've never really liked saying 'no' to buying things myself."

Christine chuckled, as she knew all about Susan's penchant for indulging herself with shopping sprees and other goodies.

"So Ryan is doing this, too?" Susan asked.

"Yep. He gets the same numbers off the computer as I do," said Christine. "But Ryan prefers to see things in black and white. He prints out a summary report and places it in his day planner. Either way, we both have the same information with us when we need it."

"Hmm."

"So enough about high finance," Christine said. "How's Rob doing? Is he still working crazy hours?"

"You know how he is. Once he got his promotion, he started working even harder to show his boss that he deserved it. Of course, he hasn't been too happy with me lately."

"Oh, why not?

"He's worried about all the credit cards we've got now, and all the balances we're carrying. But with the money he's making, I don't see how that will be a problem for long."

"Have you ever gone over the budget with him to find out how you're really doing?"

Susan shrugged. "Not really. Rob has always managed the finances. I know he's worried about how much we've saved for Megan's college education–and Danny's education and our retirement–but after all, we're still young . . . "

"Megan enters college in four years, Susan. Are you guys going to be all right?"

"I know we should have more saved by now," she said, "but I really think Rob's new raise will make a big difference."

"I'm sure it will help, Susan," said Christine, a little more seriously now. "But one of the things we learned the hard way is that if you're not tracking your expenditures, you really can't know whether you're spending more than you're earning."

"I'm sure I'm not spending more than we make," Susan said, a little uncertainly. "And Rob hardly spends anything at all–he's so stingy."

"Well, when Ryan and I did the numbers, we found out that we had been consistently spending about 10 percent more than we were making over the past three years."

"But surely not since you returned to work?"

Christine nodded. "Yeah, I was a little shocked to learn that as well."

"I don't know, Christine," she said. "I already have Rob looking over my shoulder and second-guessing every purchase I make. I just don't like the idea of watching every nickel. I can't live like that."

"Would you rather have Rob mad at you all the time?" Christine asked. "Ryan and I were snipping at each other over this stuff all the time, and it really was wearing on us both until we figured it out."

Susan nodded, "I know you're right, Christine."

"I mean, if not for your own future, think about Megan and Danny's. Megan's taking all of those AP classes now; she's probably going to get into a really good college. But will you and Rob be able to afford it?"

Susan sighed and put down her fork. She knew Christine was right, but she hated the idea of having to pinch pennies. Just then, Danny ran up to her, with Chad and Jennie trailing behind. "Mommy! Mommy!" he yelled. "I saw an F-14 fighter kit in the store, can I get it? It's only $15."

Susan just looked at Christine sheepishly, then turned to Danny and said, "I don't know, honey."

■ ■ ■ ■ ■

Two weeks later, Ryan and Christine entered Tom's office for their one-month visit.

Shirley waved them to some chairs. "Tom will be with you guys shortly. So, tell me, how's the system working for you?"

"Really well so far, Shirley," said Christine. "You were right. Using the envelope budgeting system feels very natural to me now. I can't imagine going back to doing things the way we did before."

"That's for sure," said Ryan. "I've been amazed at how painless it is. I thought it would be much harder to use than it is."

"I'm so glad it's working out for you guys," said Shirley. "This next step is going to be fun. Tom's going to show you how you can start to put money away using the system."

The door opened, and Tom walked out, bidding farewell to a client. Then he invited Ryan and Christine into his office. "You're still coming over on Saturday, right Shirley?" asked Christine.

"I wouldn't miss it," she said. "I'll talk to you later, OK?"

Ryan and Christine walked into Tom's office. "Have a seat," Tom said, pulling out a chair for Christine. "So, how are you doing using the envelope budgeting system?"

Ryan gave Tom a rundown on their last four weeks. He presented Tom with a copy of their balanced spending plan, including their net monthly income, envelope spending accounts, and the amount they were allocating to each.

Tom sat back in his chair, carefully reviewing the report. After a few minutes, he smiled and asked, "How does it feel to know you were able to live within your net monthly income for a month?"

"It has been an exhilarating experience," Christine responded quickly.

Ryan added, "I honestly didn't think we could do it after we defined the balanced spending plan, but the numbers tell the story. It feels great to be much more in control financially."

Tom placed the summary report on the table and started highlighting a few of the envelope spending accounts the two of them had created. While marking the report, he asked them a few additional questions about their envelope experience. He wanted to know how well they were communicating and how much the real-time tracking information was helping them with daily decision making.

Ryan and Christine took turns providing answers to his questions. It was easy for them to respond, because the two of them had spent a lot of time discussing these very things over the past four weeks.

When Tom finished marking their report, he leaned back in his chair and said, "You two are to be commended. You have done better with an envelope budgeting system in the first four weeks than some I've worked with. You are definitely on the right track."

"That's good to hear," said Ryan.

"One thing I would like to do today is to share some information about debt. Then I would like to talk with you about developing a strategy to rapidly eliminate your consumer debt. Did you know that there are more than three billion credit card offers mailed out each year?"

"I think we get a billion at our house alone," laughed Christine.

"Partly as a result, studies show that the collective debt of Americans now totals nearly 110 percent of total annual net income. That's up from about 85 percent in the early 1990s. Even though people know they owe money, they still go out to eat—and charge their dinner to the future. Over the holidays, fully two-thirds of Americans planned to make one or more purchases with plastic."

"Sure, but most of them are planning to pay off their credit cards, aren't they?" asked Ryan.

"They have good intentions, but often they don't ever manage to do it. Our collective consumer debt continues to rise every year in this country. In fact, according to the Economic Policy Institute, a think tank based in Washington, D.C., the biggest story of the 1990s wasn't a bullish stock market but the rising debt burden for the typical household. Look at this." Tom pulled out a sheet of paper. "People begin to get in too deep by first maxing out their home equity line, then borrowing against their retirement savings, and finally seeking a consolidation loan." He set the paper down. "People want a quick fix, and there isn't one. However, I have found that if I require prospective clients to first change their spending habits, I can help them start successfully down the path to financial fitness. I recommend an envelope budgeting system, because it allows people to manage their spending and make better choices without ongoing help from me. And I can see you're already finding the benefits."

"Yes, we are. We've been able to spend more time talking productively about our money in these past few weeks than ever before," said Ryan.

"Now I'd like to show you how to use the system to accelerate your debt elimination. Let's take a look at your spending plan." For the next several minutes, the three of them discussed several of the envelope spending accounts. After discussing a few changes in funding amounts for some of the accounts, Tom said, "I suggest you transfer the money left in your monthly discretionary envelope accounts, like groceries, eating out, and recreation, to your debt-reduction or savings envelope accounts before the next month's funding takes place."

"Why? Don't we need to build them up a bit first?" asked Ryan.

"Only if you feel you need to spend more next month in those areas than you did this month. Otherwise, you've already found out that you can stay within the monthly limits you set for these accounts. Now, take the difference and apply it toward debt reduction and savings."

FIGURE 4.1 ■ Success Cycle Implementation

Success Cycle Implementation

Make necessary adjustments, including envelope-to-envelope transfers

PLAN

Define income, create envelope spending accounts, allocate income

ADJUST

Financial Fitness

TRACK

Compare actual spending to the plan

COMPARE

Download and assign, or manually track, all transactions

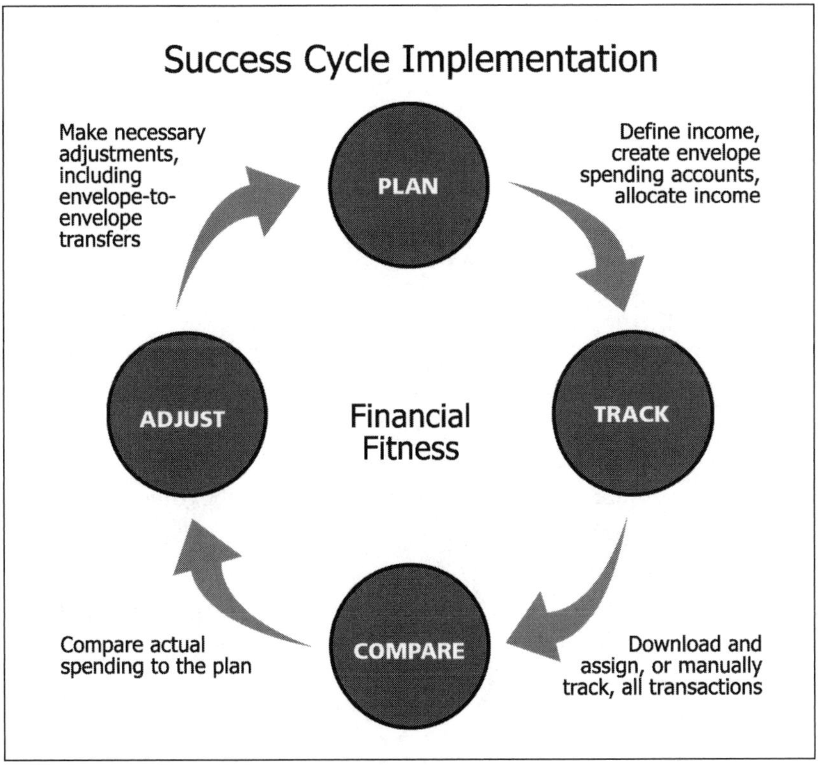

Tom reached for the Success Cycle chart on his desk. "I want to review this with you again quickly." He placed the chart on the table and pointed to the steps PLAN, TRACK, COMPARE, and ADJUST. Ryan and Christine looked at the chart as Tom continued. "After you make the adjustments we have been discussing, you will have completed one cycle in the first month. You first created your plan," Tom said, as he pointed to the copy of their original spreadsheet. "Next, you began tracking your progress. You did this every time you recorded your new transactions and assigned them to the proper envelope spending accounts, which updated the balance in each account. Finally, with the help of the latest report you made, we have just completed the comparison step. You can make the necessary adjustments when you return home today." (See Figure 4.1.)

Tom sat back and smiled. "Every month when you complete this cycle, you will get better at eliminating unnecessary spending. As you

FIGURE 4.2 ■ Richardsons' Debt Obligations

Richardsons' Debt Obligations

Description	Balance	Payment	Interest Rate
Department Store	$435	$75	21.00%
Visa	$4,350	$95	18.50%
American Express	$4,855	$75	14.50%
Auto Loan	$14,750	$517	8.90%
Home Equity Line	$9,875	$142	8.50%
Student Loan	$3,950	$142	7.50%
Mortgage	$206,320	$1,422	7.00%

continue to repeat this cycle, you will eventually become financially independent."

"We've got a long way to go," observed Ryan.

"Perhaps. But I'd like to show you how you can accelerate that process once you have stopped overspending. As long as you are not accumulating additional debt, you can begin reducing your existing debt very quickly using a technique called the 'debt roll-down principle.'" Tom pulled out a sheet of paper and said, "Let's first list all of your debt obligations, along with their current balance, minimum monthly payment, and annual interest rate."

Ryan and Christine helped Tom list each of their debt obligations on a sheet of paper.

"The next step," Tom said, "is to prioritize the payment of each of these debts. Generally, the easiest way to do this is by looking at the annual interest rate. First on the list would be the debt with the highest interest rate. In this case, it's your department store account, followed by your Visa account. The last debt on the list is the one with the lowest interest rate–your mortgage." (See Figure 4.2.)

Tom continued, "The idea behind the debt roll-down principle is to set aside a certain amount for debt repayment, then continue to maintain the total monthly amount you pay in debt reduction even after the first debt is paid off. Simply apply the amount you were paying on the first debt to the next debt on the list. When that debt too is paid off, you apply the amount you had been paying on one and two to the

FIGURE 4.3 ■ Richardsons' Debt Calculation Report

Richardsons' Debt Calculation Report

Current Debt Pay-off:

total pay-off time:	26 years 10 months
total interest paid:	$265,589

Using Envelopes Budgeting and the Debt Roll-down Principle:

total pay-off time:	13 years 8 months
total interest paid:	$142,163

Total Interest Savings:	$123, 426
Total Reduction in Time:	13 years 2 months

third, and so on. The key here is to make sure you continue paying the same aggregate amount every month until every debt is paid.

"Now," Tom continued, looking directly at them, "let's apply this technique to the envelope spending system. You have already set up an envelope spending account for each of your debt obligations. The amount of funding you are applying each month is equal to the payment you make for each debt. As soon as you pay off the first debt, transfer the funding for that envelope to the next highest priority debt envelope. When that one too is paid off, transfer the combined funding to the next highest priority debt envelope, and so on until you have eliminated all of your debt–including your mortgage."

Tom reached for his laptop computer. "Just for fun, I'm going to quickly enter your current debt into a debt calculator. This calculator will determine how soon you will be completely out of debt using this principle."

Tom found the calculator and entered the required information. He then printed the report for Ryan and Christine. As the two of them looked at the tables, they couldn't believe it. If they followed this principle, they could be completely debt free, including their mortgage, in about 14 years. (See Figure 4.3.)

"What's more," Tom said, "you'll literally save tens of thousands of dollars in interest. Imagine living without the burden of debt. Imagine how much money you could save and invest if you were not paying interest!"

Tom smiled at the two of them and said, "Earlier, we talked about being able to save approximately 10 percent of your monthly income by actively using the envelope spending principles. If you really want to move through your debt quickly, at the end of each month transfer the amount remaining in each discretionary envelope to the highest priority debt payment envelope. This added amount is called an accelerator. Let me show you the impact of using an accelerator."

Tom looked again at the amount of Ryan and Christine's net monthly income. "Your net monthly income is $6,236. If you were able to save an additional 10 percent, that would be $624. Let's plug that number into the debt calculator and look at the impact it has." Tom entered the number and printed the new report. As he looked at the report, he said, "This is when it gets really exciting." Tom handed the report to Ryan and Christine and watched their reaction.

"You mean to tell us that if we also use an accelerator with envelopes and the roll-down principle, we can be completely out of debt in 8 years and 11 months?" Ryan asked cautiously. (See Figure 4.4.)

"That's right," Tom answered confidently. "If you continue using envelopes with the debt roll-down principle as I have outlined, while looking for every opportunity to save, you will be debt free in just under nine years, as the report suggests."

Ryan looked at Christine and said, "That's unbelievable! I would not have thought in a million years that we would be able to accomplish that feat in so short a time."

"After using an envelope system for just four weeks," said Christine, "I can see how it might be possible now." She looked at Ryan, "Honey, do you realize that with this timetable, we'd be out of debt by the time Chad is a senior in high school?"

"Wow," he said, "that would be something, wouldn't it?"

"OK," said Tom. "I can see you're both excited. Now it's up to you. Let's talk again in another month."

▪ ▪ ▪ ▪ ▪

FIGURE 4.4 ■ Richardsons' Debt Calculation Report with Accelerator Payments

Richardsons' Debt Calculation Report With Accelerator Payments

Current Debt Pay-off:

total pay-off time:	26 years 10 months
total interest paid:	$265,589

Using Envelopes Budgeting and the Debt Roll-down Principle, with an Accelerator:

monthly accelerator:	$624
total pay-off time:	8 years 11 months
total interest paid:	$86,195

Total Interest Savings:	$179, 394
Total Reduction in Time:	17 years 11 months

Ryan and Christine said good-bye to Tom and Shirley and picked up Chad and Jennie on their way to see Ryan's parents for dinner. It was a warm Friday evening, and both Ryan and Christine were looking forward to the chance to unwind after a long workweek.

Christine asked Chad and Jennie about their day at school and about what their friends were doing. "Grandpa is going to be cooking hamburgers out on the grill tonight," she told them. "How's that sound to you?" Chad and Jennie cheered.

"Will Grandma make potato salad?" Jennie asked.

"I'm sure she will, sweetie."

Ryan's mother, Patty, waved to the children from her porch, as they ran out of the car after it had parked in the driveway. Chad and Jennie raced up the steps to give their grandmother hugs and kisses, followed by Ryan and Christine who greeted her with Christine's homemade peach pie.

"How are you, Mom?" asked Ryan.

"Looking forward to retirement," she quipped.

"Not much longer now, right?" Ryan said.

"Well, I guess that depends on how our funds do," she said. "The way they've been going, we might never stop working." Patty smiled to show Ryan she was just kidding.

"How's Dad doing?" he asked.

"He's doing fine," she said. "He's out back just now, about to get the fire started."

Patty led Ryan, Christine, and the kids into the backyard, where they all greeted Grandpa. While the kids were running around, Patty and Christine got their iced tea and took drinks to John and Ryan. As John prepared to light the charcoal, Patty asked, "Who wants to come in the kitchen with me and help make the potato salad?"

"I do! I do!" Chad and Jennie shouted in unison. Christine joined them, so that Ryan and his father would have a chance to chat.

"So, are you looking forward to retirement, Dad?" Ryan asked. "Less than a year to go."

"Yeah, if I'm able to retire," John said.

"'*If*?" said Ryan. "Mom was saying something about never being able to retire a little bit ago. Are your mutual funds really in such bad shape?"

"Well, we got hit pretty hard the past couple of years," he said. "We're still carrying a lot of debt, and we were counting on those investments to provide a cushion for us."

"You and Mom still have a lot of debt?" Ryan was shocked.

His father shrugged.

"But the house is paid off, isn't it?"

"Not yet," his father said. "Twelve years ago, we had to take a second mortgage out on it when we got behind on our debts. That's when we started to put some more money away for our retirement, but we still have a lot of bills to pay."

Ryan couldn't see how this was possible. He knew that his parents had always enjoyed spending their money–taking trips, buying new cars and a motorboat, fine furniture, and nice clothes–but they were a year away from retiring! If his parents were still having the same problems he and Christine had had, how were they ever going to manage living on a fixed income? Although Ryan knew his father would not want his help when it came to advice on how to manage his money, he wanted to do something. He and Christine had just turned a corner, and if he could help his folks with what he'd learned, he felt like he owed them at least that much.

"Dad," Ryan said, "have you ever looked at your budget? How you're spending your money? Because Christine and I just started a new envelope budgeting system that is really working well for us."

John sipped his drink while he fiddled with the coals in the grill. "We've got a process we use," he said. "It works fine. We just have to work harder at sticking to it, that's all. I've got it under control, Ryan."

His father made it clear he wasn't interested in talking about it any further. But Ryan knew that their situation was anything but "under control."

After dinner, Ryan helped his mother with the dishes and had a chance to talk with her alone. "You know, Mom, I was talking to Dad earlier about your retirement plans," he began. "Aren't you worried a little bit about carrying so much debt going into this time of your life?"

"Well, of course I am, dear," she said.

"I offered some help, but Dad didn't seem too keen on my advice."

"Well, you know how your father is," she said.

"I know, but don't you have a say in any of this?" asked Ryan. "I mean, it's your retirement, too. Do you really want to have to keep working?"

"Not really, no."

"I think we could help if you let us," Ryan continued. "Christine and I have been working with a financial advisor who's been helping us get a handle on our spending habits. We track all of our expenses, including our credit card purchases and automatic withdrawals, using the principles of a traditional envelope budgeting system. I've been amazed at how easy it's been to use–and it's already starting to make a difference for us."

"Envelopes, huh?" his mother said. "My old Aunt Lucille used to use some kind of envelope system. She had envelopes stuffed with cash for just about everything."

"Right, it's the same idea. The system we use doesn't require us to carry cash, but the principles work just the same. It could really help you and Dad with your spending, and that would enable you to eventually take care of your debt," said Ryan.

"Well, it sounds interesting, dear," said his mother. "But your father's always managed the finances for us, and I'm not sure I want to get involved in all that."

"Mom," Ryan said, "you're involved whether you want to be or not."

"Hmm," she said, nodding, and handed him a dish to dry.

■ ■ ■ ■ ■

The next weekend, Ryan and Christine were lounging on their back deck, while Chad and Jennie kicked an old soccer ball around the yard.

Ryan took a sip of the lemonade Christine had made that afternoon and looked out at Chad and Jennie playing in the yard. "You know," he said to Christine, "I can't remember when I felt this relaxed. Probably not since we were in college."

"That *was* a while ago," Christine teased. "I think our money management has a lot to do with it. We don't have the same daily worries hanging over our heads—and we know where we stand with our finances."

"You're right," said Ryan. "I feel like we're finally keeping our heads above water—without having to struggle to do it. You know," Ryan turned his head to Christine, "I hate to spoil the moment with more money talk, but maybe tonight we could go over our debt roll-down plan."

"I was actually thinking the same thing," said Christine. "Now that we're confident we can continue to use our envelope budgeting system, I'm anxious to start reducing our debt even faster and start saving. We could do it after we put the kids to bed."

Later that evening, after Chad and Jennie were in bed, Ryan and Christine sat down in front of the office computer to go over their plan to eliminate debt in a little under nine years. "According to our spreadsheet, last month we managed to spend 2 percent less than what we earned," said Ryan.

"Considering we had been spending about 10 percent more than we were earning," said Christine, "I'd say that's incredible."

"The challenge now is for us to reduce our spending an additional 8 percent," Ryan said, looking over the numbers. "And I think I know of at least a couple of spending accounts we could cut back on even more."

"I know," said Christine, "I've been thinking about that, too. I'm sure we could reduce our spending in at least three areas."

"Well," said Ryan, "let's take a look."

Ryan and Christine proceeded to identify areas of discretionary spending that could be reduced even more—by making a few changes in what they purchased and how they took advantage of coupons and sales, they were able to reduce their groceries and clothing envelopes. By making a few low-cost improvements to the house–getting a programmable thermostat and adding a motion sensor for their outdoor lights–they realized they could save on their monthly electric and gas bills. They even looked into their phone and Internet service providers to see if they could save money there–and they could. Finally, by reducing the amount of money they spent on vacations, dining out, and entertainment, they got to the number they were looking for.

"That's it," said Ryan, "we've reduced our monthly expenditures by about $625 less than our income, just over 10 percent to put toward our debt reduction."

"It's hard to believe we could be so ruthless, where before we had so much trouble," Christine said.

"And if it doesn't work out," Ryan pointed out, "we have the ability to track our spending, compare it to the plan, and adjust accordingly."

"It is a lot easier," said Christine, "when you have a concrete goal in mind."

"And," added Ryan, "the tools to achieve it."

■ ■ ■ ■ ■

Ryan's best friend Rob Goldman stared at the little white ball sitting on the tee, wiggled the club head a few times, took a full backswing, and struck the ball, sending it slicing down the right side of the fairway.

"Dang it!" Rob exclaimed.

"Save a slice for me," said Ryan, laughing along with their two golfing buddies, Stan, a doctor, and Glenn, a local Realtor.

"Yeah, yeah," said Rob, "I seem to remember your last drive bouncing off a tree and getting lost in the rough." Of the four of them, only Stan was a serious golfer. Ryan and Rob played about once a month to relax, although lately Ryan had cut back to every other month.

Glenn teed off and hit a looping drive into the left fringe of the rough. Stan eyed his shot carefully, reared back, and hit the ball on a line straight down the middle of the fairway. Ryan's tee shot landed about 15 yards from where Rob's had landed.

"Looks like we're in it together, buddy," laughed Rob.

After Ryan and Rob found their balls and hit their second shots, they walked back up the fairway together. Rob asked how Ryan and Christine were doing, and Ryan asked Rob about Susan and the kids.

"I hear Megan's doing really well in school, that must be exciting," said Ryan.

"She's always been such a good student," Rob said. "And they have some really fine teachers at the high school she attends."

"So, have you started thinking about colleges yet?" asked Ryan. "It's got to be hard to imagine—I can still remember when Megan was just a baby."

"Ugh, college," said Rob with a sigh. "Don't remind me. I still have to figure out how we're going to swing that. Do you know how much tuition costs these days? And I'm just talking about *state* schools."

"I know, I know. At least Christine and I have more time to prepare for it," said Ryan. "Of course, who knows how much tuition will be in ten years?"

"True. I always thought there'd be enough time to prepare, but we just haven't been able to save the way I hoped we would. I've tried to work with Susan on our budget, but I just haven't had the time lately to keep tabs on things, and she's always resisted my trying to limit her spending. So I end up feeling like I'm just nagging her."

"Believe me, Rob, I know how hard that can be on your relationship."

"It's not just college, though," Rob continued. "We haven't put away anything for our retirement, except the little that's in my 401(k). I've tried to explain all this to Susan, but I just think it doesn't seem real to her. She has all her credit cards, and if one's maxed out, she just moves on to another one."

"You might want to try the system that Christine and I started using recently," said Ryan. "It makes it really easy to manage your spending, because it helps you track your expenses on a daily basis. Christine and I can talk about our budget together now without getting upset at each other, or ourselves. The principles of the system have taught us that focusing more attention on our purchasing habits can save us quite a bit of money . . . and heartbreak, for that matter."

"That sounds great," said Rob. "But I doubt Susan would ever use it."

"Well, I mean, I love to spend money," said Ryan, "so I never thought I'd be crazy about putting limits on my spending. But once you try it for a while, you like the feeling of having power over your money, of not feeling helpless—and of building up a nest egg."

"Well, I'll think about it."

"Here it is," said Ryan, as he came to a stop in front of Rob's ball. "It's your shot."

■ ■ ■ ■ ■

It was the two-month mark, and Ryan and Christine were on their way to meet with Tom to discuss their progress so far. They'd both come a long way, and were even beginning to implement their accelerated debt roll-down plan. They were excited to share their progress with Tom.

When Ryan and Christine walked into the office, they saw Shirley and started sharing the good news.

"Have you started your debt roll-down program yet?" Shirley asked.

"We created our plan about three weeks ago and have just begun to put it into action," said Christine. "Shirley, you must be an old pro at this by now. How long have you been using an envelope budgeting system?"

"For about three years now," she said. "Soon after the divorce, I found myself with more debt than I knew what to do with, and even when Russell was able to pay the child support, it wasn't nearly enough to do anything about the money I owed. When I came to work for Tom, he really helped me understand how I could control my spending with an envelope system."

"Three years, wow. So, have you been using cash envelopes this whole time?" asked Ryan.

"Well, when I first started, I learned how to use it the old-fashioned way, with some help from a good spreadsheet. Gradually, more sophisticated tools came along that allowed me to track my spending automatically in real time."

"That's fantastic, Shirley," said Christine.

"When I first started using the envelope budgeting system with Tom, we figured out that it would take me a little over 12 years to pay down all of my debt. Once I worked on reducing my spending by another 8 percent, I was on track to eliminate my debt within seven years. I've been doing it for three years, and I'm nearly halfway home."

Ryan and Christine just looked at each other and smiled.

Just then, Tom opened the door to his office and called over to Ryan and Christine, "Hey, you two, come on in. I can't wait to hear how you're doing."

■ ■ ■ ■ ■

Christine set out some salads. "Hurry up, Ryan, the Goldmans will be here any minute."

"I'm coming. Where do you want these bowls?"

"Just set them on the table next to the plates."

The doorbell rang, and then the door opened. "Hello. Anyone home?" called Susan.

"In here," called Christine.

"Here's a cake," said Susan, coming in through the front door. "Where do you want it?"

"On the counter. We'll save it for later, when we get out the games."

Susan and Rob, along with their two children, Megan and Danny, filed into the kitchen, saying their hellos and how-are-yous. Rob lifted the lid on Christine's Crock-Pot. "Barbecued spare ribs. Yum."

"Go sit down. We're ready to eat."

Rob quickly grabbed a chunk of meat, then let the lid fall. "Yikes! It's hot!"

"Serves you right," said Christine. "Come on, time to feed the hungry masses."

During dinner, Ryan turned to Rob. "So what are you working on these days?"

"I'm writing a program that'll earn us a million bucks."

"Oh, yeah?" said Ryan.

"Yes," said Susan, "of course, in the meantime, we never get to see him."

"Right, I know you miss me," said Rob. "So you console yourself by buying shoes."

"Hey, they were on sale!" said Susan.

"Yeah, marked down from $250 to $125."

"Well, that's half off. You don't want me going around dirty and barefoot, do you?"

"You could fill a swimming pool with the shoes in her closet," Rob said, smiling to Ryan and Christine.

Susan rolled her eyes. "Someone has to enjoy the money you earn," she joked. "Anyway, let's change the subject. Who's on for games? Let's get this mess cleaned up." She stood up and began clearing the table.

"Can we play?" asked Chad.

"Sure, sport," said Ryan. "We'll play one game with you kids, then you let Mom and Dad play a game with Rob and Susan."

"I want to go first!" yelled Jennie.

"No, it's my turn. You got to play first last time."

"Did not."

"Did too."

"Stop it. We'll let Danny go first."

"Aw."

They played with the children for a while, and then Megan took them into the family room and settled them down with a video while she watched them. Back in the living room, the parents began a board game.

"You know what we need?" suggested Susan. "A weekend away. Just the four of us."

"Cheap, though," added Rob.

"One night, even. We could get a motel on the beach and just relax for a day," Susan said.

"I think she's serious," Rob responded.

"I think it sounds like a lot of fun." Christine picked up a game card.

"A real break from all the stress," said Susan. "It would likely cost only a couple hundred dollars for two exotic days and a night at a seaside inn."

"So who has $200?" asked Rob.

"Forget the cost," Susan declared. "Sometimes you just have to live a little. Come on, what about it, you guys? We could plan for, say, early April."

Ryan and Christine exchanged a knowing look, and Ryan pushed back his chair. "Honey, I'll go check my planner. Does anyone need anything while I'm up?"

"I could use another Coke," Rob said with a wink, and Ryan sauntered out of the room.

Ryan found his day planner in the office and reviewed the current spending envelopes. As he expected, the vacation envelope wasn't nearly as full as it needed to be. He made some quick calculations. *With the kids staying with my parents that weekend and with us gone for two days,* he thought, *we could reduce what we spend on groceries that week and move that money over to the vacation envelope. And, if we reduce our personal expenses, we might just be able to make this work. Still, we'll have to cut back on entertainment until then. It's a bit of a sacrifice, but we do need the break. It's worth it.*

Ryan grabbed Rob's drink and a bowl of chips from the kitchen on his way back to the living room. He handed Christine the spreadsheet with his adjustments in the margins.

"So, did you check your schedule?" Susan asked.

"Well, sort of . . . this is part of our new budgeting system," Ryan explained and turned to Christine. "Honey, I think we can make this work if we can cut back on some personal expenses and entertainment. Does that work for you, or do you want to plan for that money differently?"

"You know, if we could wait a month," said Christine while she studied the paper, "then there would be enough in the 'vacation' envelope without having to cut on personal items. But you're right, we'll have to tighten the entertainment budget a bit."

Christine looked up at her friends. "OK, we're on, if we can wait until May, and if you guys don't mind skipping over us for dinner and a movie a few times until then."

Ryan agreed. "That's a good month to take a short trip, and we can make our reservations now."

Rob didn't say anything. He just looked at Ryan. "You got it all paid for, and we haven't even left!"

Ryan looked at Christine and smiled.

"I know it may seem a little odd," said Ryan, "because we never used to manage our money very carefully. But we've gotten really used to using this envelope budgeting approach. It's becoming very natural to us now."

Susan was amazed at how Ryan and Christine could openly discuss money and spending without snipping at each other. Although she'd suggested the trip, she really didn't know whether or not she and Rob could afford it. Deep down, Susan knew that she'd feel a whole lot better if she could still buy the things she liked without having to wonder what it might be doing to their overall financial health.

"Honestly," said Christine, "it's not as tough as it looks."

Actually, it looks easier than what we've been doing, thought Susan.

■ APPLIED PRINCIPLE 11

Use an envelope budgeting system to track every expense.

Completing your monthly spending *plan*—the first step on the Success Cycle—is a critical step toward achieving financial fitness. This plan will provide direction for making spending decisions throughout the month. However, like all things, ultimate success requires persistent execution. The envelope system requires careful tracking to ensure accurate information. The bulk of this effort comes through carefully *tracking* all spending during the month—the second step on the Success Cycle. Tracking every expense can seem daunting at first, but with the help of the right tools, this task can become simple, even automatic. The most critical component to successful tracking is the proactive decision to do it. Once you have made the decision to track every expense, you can begin to review the implementation tool that will work best for you. At first, Ryan and Christine were concerned about tracking every expense, but they trusted Tom's opinion and made a mutual decision to do it. Tom then introduced them to some tools that made tracking each expense much simpler than they thought.

Tracking all of your spending is quite simple with a cash-based envelope system, as every transaction is automatically subtracted from the balance remaining in a particular spending envelope, or account. For example, when you make a clothing purchase, you take the clothing envelope with you and pay for the purchase from the clothing envelope. Let's say you have $100 left in your clothing envelope, and you are making a $60 purchase. When you hand the cashier the $60, you will have $40 left in the envelope. In the case of the cash-based envelope system, spending and tracking take place at the same time. Remember, the key is to always know how much is left to spend. You now know that you have $40 left to spend in your clothing envelope. This amount of money will need to last until you again allocate money to that envelope from the receipt of future income. (See Figure 4.5.)

If you use a paper-based system, you will need to record the non-cash spending transaction—that is, check, debit card, or other—in your bank account register as well as your clothing account register and subtract that amount from the $100 balance in the clothing account. The same would be true if you created an account register spreadsheet on the computer. If you are using a fully automated envelope-based computer system, your transaction will be tracked for you. You will simply need to download the non-cash transaction and assign it to your cloth-

FIGURE 4.5 ■ Tracking Spending with a Cash-Based Envelope System

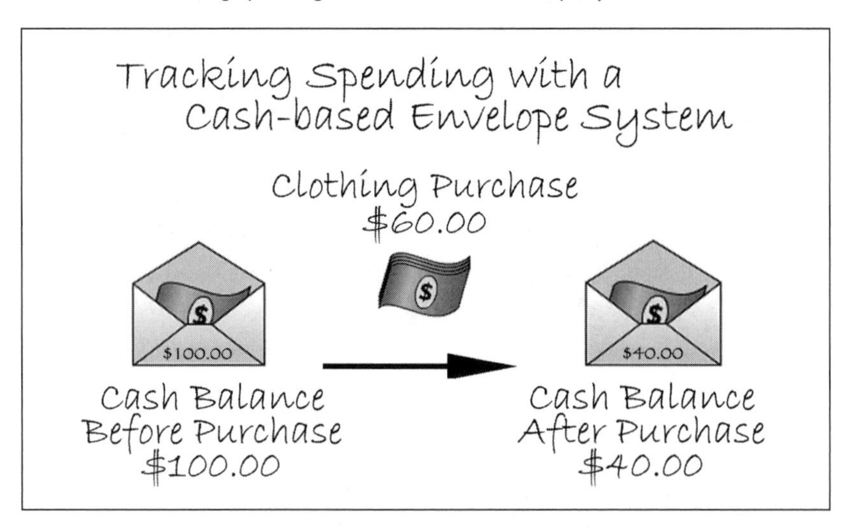

ing spending account. The system will automatically update the balance remaining in that account for you. Appendix B on page 155 provides more detail on each of these systems and how they can be used.

The major problem with most budget systems is that they provide after-the-fact information, meaning you create a plan in advance and determine the amount you will spend in each spending category. You then run a report at the end of the month, which tells you all the categories in which you have overspent. With this approach, the information is not real time—in other words, you did not have the information you needed at the time you were making a purchase decision. These systems do not tell you how much is left to spend every day. The envelope budgeting system provides this critical information.

Even with the significant advantages of the envelope budgeting system, it is only as good as your determination to use it. Meticulous tracking will only prove successful if you are prepared to guide your spending decisions based on the information the envelope system is providing you. Most people are very successful at making solid purchase decisions when they know how much is left to spend. But ultimately, your success in making sound decisions will depend on your resolve to live within your means. Ryan and Christine soon found it much easier to make informed decisions when they started tracking each expense. Their decision to travel with Rob and Susan was a result of having accurate information. Christine's positive discussion with Jennie at the zoo was facilitated by having up-to-date spending information.

■ APPLIED PRINCIPLE 12

Make appropriate spending decisions.

One of the most often-cited objections to the idea of budgeting is the thought that budgets become restrictive and frustrating. The feeling that they cannot make purchases when they would like to can be very disconcerting for many people. However, in reality, as you spend beyond your income resources, your spending choices become increasingly more restricted. Real, long-lasting choice comes from making the decision to live within your means.

That said, there are many times when making a decision to spend beyond the current resources in a spending account is just fine. Let's say that a desired clothing purchase was $125. You recall the balance in the clothing envelope is $100. In this case, you have to decide if you would like to put off the purchase until you have more money in the clothing envelope, purchase a less expensive item of clothing, or transfer money from another envelope to cover the added cost. As you can see, the information provided with the envelope system has truly empowered you to make an informed decision.

Making the decision to transfer money from another envelope is not a problem, because you have made a decision to spend less in that area. For example, let's say you have $200 in your entertainment envelope and decide to transfer $25 into the clothing envelope to cover the added cost of the purchase. When you transfer this money, write a note on each envelope to record the transfer. When using the ledger or spreadsheet system, you need to show that you have transferred money from the entertainment spending account to the clothing account. The envelope computer system will allow you to do an envelope-to-envelope transfer. The spending account balances will then be updated automatically. Recording this transfer is very important for future comparisons and adjustments to your plan. In this case, you have decided to spend $25 less on entertainment over the next several weeks. This is clearly your decision to make. The Richardsons quickly felt empowerment and a sense of freedom resulting from their ability to make these decisions on an informed basis.

Now let's say that you did not have extra money in another envelope to transfer to the clothing envelope. In this case, if you are dedicated to living within your means, your only option is to either purchase a less expensive item or wait until you have more money in the clothing envelope. Choosing to spend the extra $25 when the resources are not available will limit your choices in the future, because you have just created debt above and beyond your monthly net income resources. This means you will be paying more interest next month and further reducing available resources to purchase the things you want or, more important, need.

■ APPLIED PRINCIPLE 13

Review your plan at least monthly.

As you begin to successfully implement comprehensive tracking and good decision making, you need to define a regular interval for the purpose of *comparing* your actual spending to your spending plan–the third step on the Success Cycle. For most people, the best interval for this comparison is monthly. You could do it more frequently, but less often than monthly may prove to be problematic. If you don't review your progress often enough, it is difficult to make the appropriate adjustments on a timely basis. This would be equivalent to checking your compass every mile versus every 100 yards. Obviously, it's very easy to get significantly offtrack if you only check each mile. After Ryan and Christine completed the first month, they met with Tom to review their spending plan and first month's spending history. Together, they made appropriate adjustments and prepared the next month's spending plan.

A monthly comparison with the envelope system requires the following steps.

STEP 1: Review your spending account balances.

The first step is to review your spending account balances. Determine how much is left in each envelope at the end of the month and how much was spent during the month. You need to make sure this calculation includes any money transferred from another envelope. Next, compare the amount spent during the month with the amount you planned to spend. During this step, you will see spending accounts for which you may need to increase your monthly allocation of income, and those for which you may be able to reduce your allocation. Remember that when you make adjustments in income allocations, you need to make sure your spending plan is still balanced. For example, if you increase the monthly allocation for the clothing spending account, you will need to decrease the allocation to another spending account or accounts by the same amount. The total amount of net monthly income must equal the total amount of spending account allocations. These adjustments will allow you to tighten your plan for the next month. (See Figure 4.6.)

FIGURE 4.6 ■ Spending Plan Adjustments

Spending Plan Adjustments

Spending Accounts	Monthly Allocation	Adjustments	Adjusted Allocation
Auto Fuel	**$225**	+ $35	***$260***
Babysitter	$30		$30
Clothing	**$175**	+ $25	***$200***
Entertainment	$95		$95
Eating Out	**$75**	- $13	***$60***
Groceries	**$400**	- $20	***$380***
Haircuts	$35		$35
Spending- Ryan	$50		$50
Spending- Christine	$50		$50
Personal Items	$50		$50
Supplies	$10		$10
Phone- House	$75		$75
Phone- Mobile	**$100**	- $25	***$75***
Books & Magazines	$10		$10
TOTAL DISCRETIONARY	**$1,380**	**$0**	***$1,380***

Often, you will find that you did not include a particular area of spending that needs to be tracked. In this case, you will need to create a new spending account. Again, remember that when you create a new spending account, you will need to reduce the allocation to other accounts by the amount you decide to allocate to the new account. (See Figure 4.7.)

At times, you will find you are no longer using a particular spending account. An example of this may be an account set up to save for the purchase of a major item. After the purchase is complete, you no longer need to set aside money for that spending account on a monthly basis. This will allow you to reallocate the income that has been going to that spending account to another account or accounts.

STEP 2: Transfer your savings and set new beginning balances.

Once you have completed the review of your spending account balances and made appropriate income allocation adjustments, you are ready to move on to the next step. Each month, you need to set the beginning balances for each account. The analysis for this process differs, depending on the type of spending account.

FIGURE 4.7 ■ Adding a Spending Account

Adding a Spending Account

Spending Account	Monthly Allocation	Adjustments	Adjusted Allocation
Dental Deductible	$25		$25
Doctor Visits Deductible	$60		$60
Birthday Gifts	$35		$35
Holiday Gifts	$75		$100
Other Gifts	$15		$15
Eye Care (NEW)		**+ $25**	***$25***
Auto Maintenance	$115		$115
House Maintenance	$75		$75
Vacation	$175		$225
Donations	$125		$125
Auto Fuel	$225		$250
Babysitter	$30		$50
Clothing	$175		$250
Entertainment	**$95**	**- $10**	***$85***
Eating Out	$75		$175
Groceries	$400		$425
Haircuts	$35		$50
Spending- Ryan	$50		$100
Spending- Christine	$50		$100
Personal Items	**$50**	**- $15**	***$35***
Supplies	$10		$20
Phone- House	$75		$100
Phone- Mobile	$100		$120
Books & Magazines	$10		$20
TOTAL	**$2,080**	**$0**	**$2,080**

Monthly required spending accounts. Let's first take a look at your monthly required spending accounts. Because the spending for these accounts is usually a fixed amount, and the spending takes place each month, your ending account balance should be zero, meaning you have spent the total amount of money set aside in that account by the end of the month. Remember, these spending accounts include things like required debt payments, some utility payments, monthly insurance payments, and so on. Unless your payment amount has changed, in which case you would need to make an adjustment in the amount of monthly allocation to that account, your beginning balance for these accounts will be zero.

Monthly discretionary spending accounts. Next, let's look at monthly discretionary spending accounts. If, at the end of the month, you have a remaining balance in these accounts, you have two choices: roll the balance over to the next month, in which case the ending balance will become the beginning balance, or transfer the remaining balance to another account and set the beginning balance to zero. These spending accounts represent an opportunity to move additional money to savings, debt repayment, or investments. For example, if you normally set aside $500 for groceries each month, and you have a balance remaining in your groceries account of $45 at the end of the month, you can transfer that amount to savings, investments, or additional debt repayments. You should feel comfortable with this transfer, because next month you will allocate another $500 to your groceries account. This amount should be enough to cover your expenses for the month. As a result, the $45 should be viewed as real savings. As you can see, by transferring the remaining balance in each of your monthly discretionary accounts and setting the beginning balance to zero, you can significantly increase the amount you are saving, investing, or adding to debt reduction.

Periodic required spending accounts. Let's next look at your periodic required accounts. The idea behind these accounts is to set aside money on a monthly basis for future required expenses. These accounts include things like annual property tax payments, periodic insurance payments, annual auto registration fees, and so on. Because you need the balance for these accounts to grow from month to month, you should roll the ending balance over, and it should become your beginning balance for the next month. As is the case with the monthly required accounts, if the amount of the payment changes, you will need to make an adjustment in the amount of income you allocate to this account each month. Remember, this will require an offsetting adjustment to another account or accounts to ensure your spending plan remains balanced.

Periodic discretionary spending accounts. Finally, let's take a look at the periodic discretionary spending accounts. These accounts include things like vacations, holiday spending, gifts, house maintenance, and so on. The objective for these accounts is also to set aside money for future spending requirements. However, because these accounts represent discretionary spending, you should constantly monitor the balances to determine if they are sufficient to address your spending needs. If you believe your spending requirements for one of these accounts or envelopes will increase in the future, you will need to determine how much more of your monthly income you should be allocating to this area. The same is true if you believe your spending requirements may be less than anticipated.

One of the ways to treat these accounts is to determine an annual requirement and continue setting money aside until the balance in the account has reached that amount. Once it has, you may choose to transfer any amount over that annual requirement to savings, investments, or debt repayment. An example of this would be your house maintenance account. Let's say that you believe you will need to spend $1,200 on house repairs and general maintenance over the next 12 months. Based on this number, you will be allocating $100 each month to the house maintenance account. Basically, you are saying that you want to have $1,200 set aside in case any repairs are necessary. If, after 13 months, the balance in this account exceeds your $1,200 annual repair estimate, because you have had little or no repair expenses, you can transfer the amount above this number to another account. Once you have reached the $1,200 limit, you will be able to transfer the $100 monthly allocation to house maintenance to another account, such as savings, investments, or debt repayment, in each subsequent month. However, you will always have the $1,200 set aside if it is required. After several months of lower-than-expected repairs, you may determine that the annual spending estimate is too high, and you can make an adjustment to the monthly allocation in your spending plan.

STEP 3: Reconcile your spending accounts and bank accounts.

If you are not using the cash-based envelope system, you will need to perform an account reconciliation at the end of each month. First, reconcile your bank accounts based on your normal procedure. When you are not using the cash envelope system, the total of your bank account balance should equal the total of all of your spending accounts. In other words, if you have $3,000 in your bank account, the combined balance of your spending accounts should equal $3,000. If adjustments are made in your bank account as a result of your reconciliation, you will need to make a corresponding adjustment to one or more of your spending accounts.

Also, if the combined balance of your spending accounts does not match your bank account balance, you will need to make an appropriate adjustment to one or more of your spending accounts.

This monthly reconciliation process will ensure that you can depend on the balance information in each of your spending accounts. This is very important when you are making purchase decisions based on this information.

■ APPLIED PRINCIPLE 14

Repeat the Success Cycle each month.

You have just completed one trip around the Success Cycle. You created your spending plan, meticulously tracked your spending, compared your spending to the plan, and made appropriate adjustments based on the information. Now that you understand this process, it is very important that you repeat it every month. Each time you compare and make adjustments, your plan will become more accurate. Every time you track expenses and make spending decisions based on the balance remaining, you will find other ways to save money. You will be surprised at how easy utilizing the envelope system and following the Success Cycle can be. During their initial 12-week experience with Tom, Ryan and Christine completed the Success Cycle three times. By the time they had made monthly adjustments for the third time, they had a very accurate spending plan. (See Figure 4.1 on page 91.)

One of the great benefits of the monthly review is the opportunity to sit together with your partner and review your progress toward financial objectives, and to recommit yourselves to reaching these objectives. Utilizing the envelope system and following the Success Cycle will bring significant amounts of harmony into your life. Being on the same financial page and working together to meet your financial objectives can be one of the most rewarding pursuits you can have as a couple. This was certainly the case for Ryan and Christine.

You may recall that the words FINANCIAL FITNESS are on the inside of the Success Cycle chart. As you continue to follow the Success Cycle on a monthly basis, you will become increasingly more financially fit. Financial fitness is a process, not a single event in time. By moving down this path, you are well on your way to achieving this objective!

■ APPLIED PRINCIPLE 15

Use an envelope system to rapidly eliminate debt.

One of the most crippling impacts to personal financial fitness is debt. Debt is every bit as damaging to your financial health as extra weight is to your physical health. Losing your debt load can be the most financially liberating thing you will ever do. Continuing to add to your debt will likely be the most financially restricting thing you can do.

To successfully tackle personal debt, the first thing you need to do is stop adding to it. There is no way to begin reducing debt and eventually eliminate it, if you are constantly increasing it by spending more than you make. Incorporating the principles necessary to live within your means is the first step to conquering personal debt. After you have been through the Success Cycle during the first month, you are prepared to begin an accelerated debt-reduction program.

This debt-reduction program is based on the debt roll-down principle to rapidly eliminate debt. Using an envelope system is the key ingredient to finding success with this approach. The debt roll-down principle works by determining the total monthly payment you can make toward debt repayment. Each time you pay off a debt, you add the payment for that debt to the monthly payment for the next priority debt. This will accelerate the rate at which this debt is paid. When the second debt is paid, you add the payment you have been making on this debt to the monthly payment for the third priority debt. This process is continued until all debt has been eliminated. The key is to continue making the same aggregate debt payment each month. Following this debt elimination principle can often assist you in eliminating all of your debt, including your mortgage, in as few as seven to eight years. (If you would like to calculate your repayment schedule using the debt roll-down principle, refer to Appendix D, page 173, for a list of Internet-based debt roll-down calculators.)

There are two ways to prioritize debt repayment: smallest outstanding balance to largest outstanding balance or highest interest rate to lowest interest rate. Because, in most cases, you will eliminate your debt faster if you begin with the debt carrying the highest interest rate, most financial advisors agree you should prioritize your repayment based on the interest rate–highest to lowest. You can quickly set up your rapid repayment plan by following these steps.

FIGURE 4.8 ■ Richardsons' Debt Obligations

Richardsons' Debt Obligations

Description	Balance	Payment	Interest Rate
Department Store	$435	$75	21.00%
Visa	$4,350	$95	18.50%
American Express	$4,855	$75	14.50%
Auto Loan	$14,750	$517	8.90%
Home Equity Line	$9,875	$142	8.50%
Student Loan	$3,950	$142	7.50%
Mortgage	$206,320	$1,422	7.00%

STEP 1: Create a list of all debt.

The first step is to create a list of all debt. This list should include the name of the debt, the current outstanding balance, the planned monthly payment, and the interest rate for each. Begin with the debt having the highest interest rate and end with the debt having the lowest interest rate. (See how the Richardsons prioritize their debt obligations in Figure 4.8.)

STEP 2: Check your monthly spending account allocations.

When you set up your initial monthly spending plan, you should have created a spending account for each debt on your list. If you have left one out, you will need to create a spending account for this debt. If you need to create a new account, remember to make appropriate adjustments in your spending plan to maintain a balanced plan. Each month, you will make your debt payments from the spending accounts you have created. After you pay off the first debt, you will need to make an adjustment by adding the monthly allocation for that debt to the monthly allocation of the spending account for the next priority debt. For example, let's say your debt with the highest interest rate is a department store credit card. The amount of your monthly payment for this debt is $75, so the amount of income you allocate each month to the de-

FIGURE 4.9 ■ Debt Roll-Down

Debt Roll-Down Example

	Department Store Account	Visa Account	MasterCard Account	Auto Loan	Mortgage
Month 1	$ 75	$ 125	$ 150	$ 500	$ 1,500
Month 2	$ 75	$ 125	$ 150	$ 500	$ 1,500
Month 3	$ 75	$ 125	$ 150	$ 500	$ 1,500
Month 4	$ 75	$ 125	$ 150	$ 500	$ 1,500
Month 5	* ↳	$ 200	$ 150	$ 500	$ 1,500
Month 6		$ 200	$ 150	$ 500	$ 1,500
Month 7		$ 200	$ 150	$ 500	$ 1,500
Month 8		$ 200	$ 150	$ 500	$ 1,500
Month 9		$ 200	$ 150	$ 500	$ 1,500
Month 10		$ 200	$ 150	$ 500	$ 1,500
Month 11		$ 200	$ 150	$ 500	$ 1,500
Month 12		$ 200	$ 150	$ 500	$ 1,500
Month 13		* ↳	$ 350	$ 500	$ 1,500
Month 14			$ 350	$ 500	$ 1,500
Month 15			$ 350	$ 500	$ 1,500
Month 16			$ 350	$ 500	$ 1,500
Month 17			* ↳	$ 850	$ 1,500
Month 18				$ 850	$ 1,500
Month 19				$ 850	$ 1,500
Month 20				$ 850	$ 1,500
Month 21				$ 850	$ 1,500
Month 22				$ 850	$ 1,500
Month 23				$ 850	$ 1,500
Month 24				$ 850	$ 1,500
Month 25				* ↳	$ 2,350

*As debt is paid off, the payment is added to the next debt payment to the right

partment store spending account for that debt is $75. Your next highest priority debt based on interest rate is a credit card. For this debt, your monthly payment is $125, so the amount of income you allocate to this credit card spending account each month is $125. After four months, you have paid off the department store debt. When you complete your monthly adjustment, you will transfer any remaining balance from the department store spending account to the credit card payment envelope. You also will adjust the monthly income allocation for the credit card spending account by adding the $75 to the $125. You will now be making a monthly payment of $200 on the credit card. This will be repeated each time a debt is paid off. Before long, you will have eliminated all of your consumer debt and will be making much larger mortgage payments. (See Figure 4.9.)

STEP 3: Accelerate your debt payment with monthly spending account transfers.

Once you have created your debt-elimination plan, you can begin to accelerate your debt repayment by transferring savings from your spending accounts to your debt repayment accounts. You may recall the earlier example of transferring the balance remaining in monthly discretionary spending accounts to savings, investments, or debt payments. Many people have found they can save an additional 10 percent each month by using an envelope system. If you have a net monthly income of $5,000, the additional amount you can save using the envelope system could be as much as $500. Imagine how quickly you can eliminate your consumer debt if you are adding 10 percent of your net monthly income to your debt payments. By doing this, Ryan and Christine were able to add approximately $600 each month to debt payments.

For most people in America, a significant portion of their net monthly income is dedicated to the payment of interest. Imagine how much money you can save and invest if you are not paying interest. For most, this would represent several thousand dollars each year. Invested properly, this additional money may make a significant difference in the lifestyle you choose later in life. Using an envelope system to successfully implement the debt roll-down principle will help you accomplish this objective.

Chapter Five

Money for Life

Ryan sat in a meeting with his boss Mike going over the details of Sierra, currently Medical One's largest project. Mike was pleased with the progress the project team was making. It was nearly the end of April. Just three weeks earlier, there had been a few red flags on Sierra, but with some hard work, Ryan and his team had been able to effectively address nearly every issue.

When they finished with the project review, Mike said, "Ryan, you're doing a great job here, and I wanted to let you know how much I appreciate all your hard work."

Ryan sat back in his chair and said with a smile, "Thanks, Mike. But I can't take all the credit. I've got a great team, and I owe most of our success to them."

"You do have a great team, Ryan, that's true. But you're the leader of that team, and you deserve a lot of the credit."

As Ryan rose to leave, his cell phone rang. "I'll catch you later," he said to Mike. As he walked to the door, he took the call. It was Rob.

"Hey, what's cooking over at Medical One?" asked the voice over the cell phone. "Have you guys started working yet today?"

Ryan laughed. "Are you kidding? You know us, we usually get a good start on things by, oh, 10:00 or 11:00," he joked. "So, are you out of bed yet?"

"Nope," Rob returned. "I'm still in my pajamas."

"Yeah, yeah," Ryan said, knowing Rob was always an early riser. He added, "You've probably already knocked down 10,000 lines of code this morning."

"No doubt," Rob quipped. "You know me, 100 lines a minute."

Ryan knew Rob was an excellent programmer. He had been with the same development company since graduating from college, and had gone from a technical assistant to one of their most senior programmers.

Finally, Rob asked, "Hey, what are you doing after work?"

"Well, Christine is going out tonight, so I have to be home by 7:00 to watch Chad and Jennie," Ryan answered. "What did you have in mind?"

Rob hesitated for a brief minute, and then he said, "I want to talk to you about finances for a few minutes. I want to know what kind of system you're using. Do you think you could meet me at Houlihan's after work for 30 minutes or so?"

Ryan smiled to himself. So Rob was curious. "As long as I'm on my way home by 6:30, I should be alright."

At 5 PM, Ryan shut down his computer and left the office. A few minutes later, he pulled into the parking lot in front of Houlihan's. Rob was already sitting at a booth inside.

They ordered drinks, and then talked about work for a few minutes. Finally, Rob confided in his friend. "Ryan, I'm not sure what you and Christine are doing differently with your money, but whatever it is, Susan and I need to be doing it, too."

"You must mean the envelopes?" asked Ryan.

"Yes," Rob responded. "So, what are these envelopes anyway? Susan and I need to figure something out. We have been struggling with finances for a long time, and it's starting to have a major impact on our relationship. Last night we had a fight about some pillows Susan bought—expensive down pillows. Later, after we had both cooled down, we talked for a long time. She told me about Christine using her handheld at the zoo, and I remembered how comfortably you two were able to budget our trip together. Do you mind if I ask you what you two are doing? Is this something new?"

Sitting forward, Ryan said, "Well, we're using the principles of a very traditional system of spending management. We've been working with a financial advisor who helped us get started with it. You have to do some work to set the system up, but we've found that it's incredibly easy to use, and it's allowed us to really get a handle on what we're spending, and what we're saving. Using these principles to track our spending on a daily basis keeps us from overspending without knowing about it."

"Wow," Rob said. "What about credit card purchases? That's where we've really gotten into trouble. They're so convenient, and we get reward points. But I don't think Susan realizes how much she's spending when she charges her purchases. We can never pay the entire balance each month. Over time, we just seem to max them out. I can't even remember how many times I've had the credit limit raised. Last month, Susan transferred the balance from one of our cards to a new card that offered an even higher spending limit—I mean, that is the *last* thing we need."

"Sounds painfully familiar," Ryan nodded his understanding.

Rob continued, "I'm always getting upset with Susan for using the cards, but to be honest, we really don't talk about our finances beyond that. A few years ago, we tried a personal financial software package. Although it helped with managing our checking account, it didn't really integrate our credit cards in a way that helped us make spending decisions."

"Envelope budgeting can handle managing credit card spending," Ryan began. "The entire philosophy is to set aside money in your checking account each time a purchase is made with a credit card."

Rob looked confused, "Do you have software to do that?"

"You can have software do it automatically, use a paper-based system, or a combination of the two," Ryan said. "Knowing you, Rob, I think it's safe to say that the software route would be the way for you and Susan to go. During setup of the software system, you create a balanced spending plan. This includes defining the amount of income you deposit in your bank account each month. You then create spending accounts, called envelopes, for each category of spending and divide your income among them. The allocations to your spending accounts cannot exceed your net monthly income."

"So you budget every penny?" asked Rob.

FIGURE 5.1 ■ Credit Cards and the Envelope Budgeting System

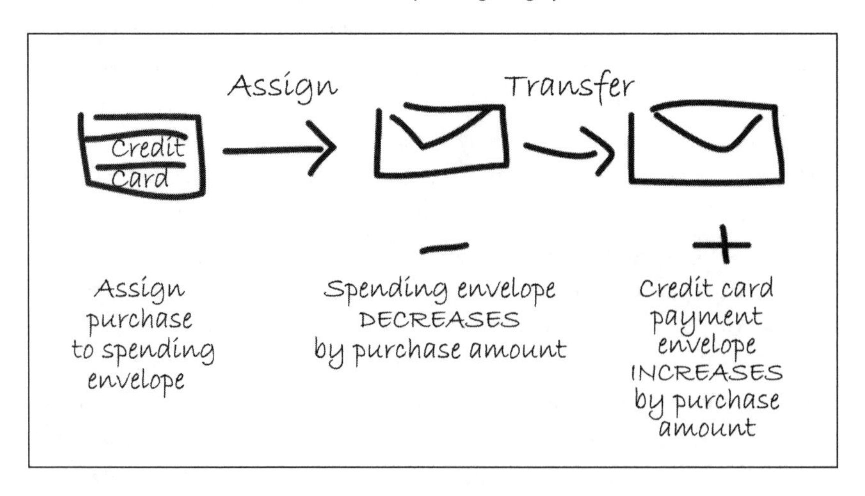

"Yes. All money is accounted for. The software tool will access your accounts, including your credit card companies. However, it does something unusual with the credit card accounts. At setup, it automatically creates a repayment account for that card."

"That's different," Rob said.

"It works really well," Ryan explained, as he took out a piece of paper and started to sketch. "When you track your transactions, including those from credit cards, you must assign each one to an envelope spending account. However, if that transaction was made with a credit card, the software subtracts the amount of that transaction from an envelope spending account and adds that amount to the repayment envelope, so the money will be there when it is needed to pay the bill." (See Figure 5.1.)

Rob looked stunned. "So, how would that work if I charged a dinner out on my card?"

Ryan replied, "Well, when you track the transaction, you assign it to, say, your 'entertainment' envelope. It will deduct the price of the dinner from that envelope and add it to the repayment envelope for that credit card."

"What if there isn't enough to cover the expense?"

"Then you stop going out to dinner for the rest of the month!" laughed Ryan. "Seriously, though, you must decide where the money will come from and transfer the difference from another account to cover it. The idea is to keep a balanced budget and live within your means. The basic envelope principle started with cash-based spending, so it was self-enforcing–you simply couldn't spend cash you didn't have. The approach we're using gives you the tools you need to enforce it yourself." Ryan paused. "When it comes to debt you already owe, you'll have to create an envelope account solely for debt reduction and allocate funds to it each month. While you pay off that debt, the envelope system will help you avoid going further into debt by making it easy to set aside the money you need each month to pay for new charges."

"Wow, that sounds like it would work really well," said Rob.

"Remarkable, isn't it?" said Ryan. "For the first time that I can remember, we have been able to successfully manage credit card spending within our monthly cash flow. Credit cards are completely integrated, and, of course, one of the major advantages is that you always know where you are with your spending plan."

Rob sat back and sipped his drink. "That's why you two went to your day planner the other night before committing yourselves to a weekend away."

"Yes. When we travel, we'll likely use our credit cards, but we must know, first, which envelope spending account will handle the transactions," Ryan said, finishing off his drink. "By applying the envelope principles, Christine and I have already been able to start reducing our consumer debt. One of our goals is to completely eliminate our consumer debt as quickly as possible." Ryan looked at his watch. "I need to take off. Let me know if you're interested, and I'll get you our financial advisor's number. Or, if you have any other questions, just give me a call. I'll be happy to provide whatever input I can. I'm sure you and Susan can turn things around."

"Thanks for taking some time with me," said Rob. "I think I'll ask Susan if she wants to sit down with me later tonight and talk about this. An envelope approach may be just what we need."

■ ■ ■ ■ ■

Ryan and Christine were on their way to meet with Tom. They had reached their 12-week milestone and felt they were making great progress. In that relatively short period of time, their envelope budgeting system had become a big part of their life. Looking back, Ryan wondered how they had ever survived without it. But then, on second thought, just surviving was exactly what they had been doing only a few months ago.

As they arrived, Tom emerged from his office with an older, African-American gentleman and his wife. "Hello, Ryan and Christine," he said, shaking hands with them. Turning to the couple with him, he said, "Let me introduce you to Walter and Lucy Howard. We have been working together for more than 30 years. They were actually one of my first clients. Walter and Lucy, this is Ryan and Christine Richardson. They came to see me about 12 weeks ago and have been using a computerized version of envelopes since then."

Extending his hand to Walter, Ryan said, "It's a pleasure to meet you both."

"Likewise," Walter responded.

Lucy shook their hands and said, "It's so nice to meet you."

"So," said Walter, "how do you like the envelope budgeting system so far?"

"It's been a big help to us," said Ryan.

"It's amazing how much these simple principles have helped," Christine added. "Are these what you've been using all these years?"

"Well, yes," said Walter. "Not with computers, but the old-fashioned way. When we first started working with Tom, we had some savings, but we also had a lot of debt. He was the one who figured out that if we could manage our spending, we could get rid of our debt and have a lot more to invest." Tom nodded and smiled.

Walter continued. "He looked into it and came back to us with the envelope budgeting system. We've been using it ever since."

"So you've found it helpful?" asked Christine.

"You could say that," said Lucy with a smile.

Tom cleared his throat and put his hand on Walter's shoulder. "Once Walter and Lucy paid down their debt," he said, "they were able to make some strategic investments. Some retail businesses downtown . . . "

"The Piggly Wiggly on 9th," said Walter, "and the Popeye's on Larabee and 12th. We also own some commercial real estate downtown and an apartment building in the Lakewood neighborhood."

"Wow," said Ryan. "Have you always been an entrepreneur?"

"No," Walter said. "Most of my career, I was a technician at the Cedar Rock power plant. Lucy was a librarian at the public library. I let others manage the businesses, but I keep an eye on each of the operations."

"That's so impressive," said Christine. "I hope we're able to do even half as well."

Walter smiled at Christine and said with a wink, "Once you save your first million, it gets really fun."

Ryan gave Christine a perplexed look, as the Howards said goodbye and walked down the hall.

"Come in and have a seat." Tom led them into his office. "Now, there's a great example of what you can accomplish when you adopt the envelope principles and continue to follow them. Walter and Lucy had modest incomes, yet by adopting the envelope principles, they stayed in control of their financial world and planned for their future."

"That's great," Ryan said. "They certainly seem to be enjoying their retirement."

"They just returned from an extended trip to California, where they were visiting their oldest son and his family. Now, they're planning a cruise in Finland." Tom sat back and looked directly at them. "They are doing exactly what they want to do. And they have the money they need to keep doing what they want to do for the rest of their lives. That's the power behind the principles you are now following."

"Just out of curiosity . . . " Ryan began.

Tom broke in, "What Walter said about their first million?"

"Yeah."

"He wasn't kidding."

Ryan and Christine looked at each other, then back at Tom, a little in shock. "A technician and a librarian," Christine said, smiling at Ryan. "Do you think we can accomplish that, honey?"

Ryan smiled back. "It might be a little early to tell, but I think we're on the right track."

Tom leaned forward in his seat. "You don't have to pull down six or seven figures to become wealthy. And, you don't have to have significant wealth to be financially fit and happy. It's all about spending less than you earn, and doing it consistently over time. If you can do it for 32 years, just imagine where you'll be." Tom paused, as his last statement sunk in with Ryan and Christine. "So how are you doing? You have been at this project for just over 12 weeks now. Tell me about your progress."

"Christine and I reviewed the numbers carefully last night, and honestly, we are amazed. First of all, we had over $1,000 in our checking account at the first of the month. That is an absolute first for us. Second, we have managed to pay off an additional $600 in consumer debt by transferring the savings from some of our envelope spending accounts at the end of each month to our debt-payment envelopes."

Christine spoke up. "When I look at how we approach things today, and our philosophy toward spending and financial management, I just can't believe the difference. It's been a very big transformation for us. I know that if we continue applying the envelope principles, we will reach our financial goals, including the complete elimination of our debt."

"Yes, you will," Tom responded.

"As we were looking over our envelope account balances last night, Christine and I decided to reward ourselves with a vacation as soon as we have reduced our consumer debt by $3,000. The great thing about envelopes is that for the first time, we will have the money set aside in advance of taking the vacation."

"It may not be as upscale as previous vacations," Christine added, "but we will know that it is paid for before we leave."

"There are few feelings better than knowing that you have money set aside for future requirements. The two of you have made exceptional progress with this system. Best of all, you have done this together without any real help from me."

"But you have been a great help to us," protested Ryan.

"I provided the introduction to the tools and philosophies you needed, and the two of you did all the work. When you make these principles a part of your daily life, the results can be extraordinary. And that's what it's all about–assisting ordinary people to achieve extraordinary financial results. You are absolutely on the right path."

"Thanks for your confidence in us," Christine responded.

"As soon as you have removed additional debt and have started accumulating more in savings," Tom said, "let's meet again and prepare a detailed financial plan for the future."

"That sounds great," Ryan said. "When we first started this project, we weren't sure it was possible to achieve the kind of results you were talking about. Now, I believe it more than ever. Living within our income and planning for our future is exactly what we want for our family."

■ ■ ■ ■ ■

Nine months after starting to use the envelope spending management system, Ryan and Christine found themselves walking hand in hand in the cool, white sand of the Caribbean. It was their second day of a weeklong vacation to St. Thomas. The early morning air was crisp and clean. Ryan found the spot he was looking for—a flat area nestled between several rocks on a small hill overlooking the surf. He set down the picnic basket and spread a blanket on the sand.

Sitting down, Christine opened the basket and began arranging things. "Thanks for bringing me to this wonderful place, sweetheart."

"We earned it. We've both worked together these last nine months to dig ourselves out of the hole we were in."

As she finished emptying the contents of the basket, Christine reached for Ryan's hand. "I think this is the most wonderful vacation we have ever taken together."

"We have certainly spent less than in the past."

"I know, but this time it's paid for. I feel so free and happy, knowing we can afford this time together."

"Do you remember last Christmas? We set a goal for ourselves . . ." Ryan reminded her.

"We did, didn't we?" Christine said with a smile. "And we found exactly what we were looking for."

■ APPLIED PRINCIPLE 16
Use credit cards appropriately.

Credit cards have become a major part of our society. Many purchases can only be made with a credit card or debit card. In the United States, only about one-third of those with credit cards pay their balance in full each month. The other two-thirds carry a balance from one month to the next. The interest rate associated with this outstanding balance generally averages about 12 percent and can sometimes exceed 25 percent. Credit cards represent a major convenience for many people but also have become a significant burden for most.

One of the biggest problems with credit card spending is that most people don't incorporate these purchases into their available monthly cash flow. As a result, purchases are made that often exceed an individual's monthly net income. Most people intend to pay the balance each month, but as the month rolls forward, they do not have the resources necessary to do so. This was the experience Ryan and Christine had. Because their monthly expenses exceeded their monthly income, there was no way they could pay for their credit card purchases in full. Yet, they always rationalized this spending. Because of the inherent problems and financial risks associated with credit card spending, many financial advisors and coaches suggest their clients not use credit cards at all. If a card is needed to pay for a hotel visit, rental car, or flight purchase, the safest card to use is a debit card, because the purchase is made from existing funds in your bank account.

If you are intent on making purchases with a credit card, the envelope system provides a method for using credit cards appropriately. The key to successful credit card spending is making sure you set aside an amount of money from your monthly net income equal to your credit card purchases, so you can pay the card balance in full each month. While it is unlikely you will be using credit cards with the cash-based envelope system, if you do, you will need to create a credit card repayment envelope for each credit card you use. Every time you make a purchase with a credit card, you take money from the appropriate envelope and place it in the credit card repayment envelope. For example, if you wanted to purchase an article of clothing from an Internet retailer for $45 using your Visa card, you would take $45 from your clothing envelope and place it in your Visa repayment envelope. When your Visa bill

FIGURE 5.2 ■ Credit Card Repayment Using the Envelope Budgeting System

Credit Card Repayment Using the Envelope Budgeting System

Assign Transfer Pay-off

CREDIT

$100.00

$0.00

CREDIT

CREDIT CARD PURCHASE $45	CLOTHING BUDGET - $45	CREDIT CARD REPAYMENT + $45	CREDIT CARD PAYMENT $45
Assign the purchase to the spending envelope	Spending envelope DECREASES from $100 to $55	Credit card repayment envelope INCREASES by $45	Make payment on credit card. New balance on credit card is $0

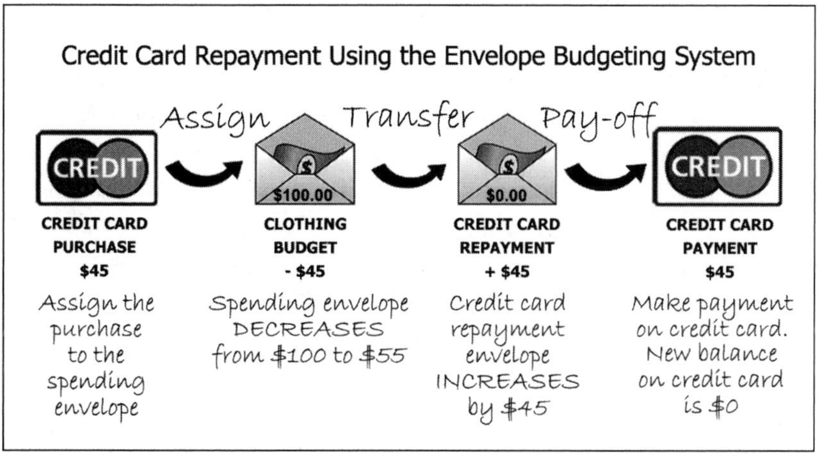

arrives, you will use the money in the repayment envelope to pay the entire balance. (See Figure 5.2.)

If you have an existing balance on your Visa card when you begin using the envelope system, you will need to allocate an amount of your monthly net income to meet the monthly payment requirements for that card. When you make your credit card payment, you will pay this monthly allocation together with an amount that represents your total card purchases for the previous month. This approach will allow you to begin reducing your credit card balance and ensure that future purchases are paid in full each month.

With the ledger, or spreadsheet, envelope method, you will need to create a repayment account for each credit card you intend to use. As credit card purchases are made, you will need to enter a transfer from the appropriate spending account to the credit card repayment account. Each month, credit card payments will be tracked on the corresponding repayment spending account ledger.

With the computer-based envelope system, the repayment account is created during your initial setup. When credit card purchases are made, transfers from the selected spending account to the appropriate repayment envelope take place automatically as you make an assignment of the transaction.

■ APPLIED PRINCIPLE 17

Make a 12-week commitment.

Any decision to change direction or refocus efforts requires courage and fortitude. Generally, resistance to change is the strongest within the first several weeks of moving down a new path. This is certainly the case for many seeking to become physically fit. How many diet and exercise programs are started and stopped before they had time to create real change? How many New Year's resolutions have been adopted and then dropped and forgotten by the end of January?

For any worthwhile change in direction to take root, an initial commitment of several weeks must be made. This initial thrust must be long enough to overcome the natural resistance you may have to change. Creating new ways of thinking and better habits also takes some time. However, in as few as 12 short weeks, a significant change in your personal financial health can take place. And, as you move down the path during this initial 12-week period, you will find it becomes easier and easier to achieve your objectives. Once your thoughts, actions, and habits become aligned with your financial fitness objectives, you will be able to achieve extraordinary things. This success comes only to those who are willing to sail through a few short weeks of stormy weather on their path to a safe financial harbor.

During the initial 12-week period, you will complete a net-worth statement, which will become a benchmark to chart your progress in the future. You will implement an envelope budgeting system, begin saving for the future, and start rapidly paying down consumer debt. You will move through the Success Cycle three times. By the time you have adjusted your monthly spending plan for the third time, you will be well on your way to consistently living within your means–the most important aspect of becoming financially fit.

Many physical fitness trainers and coaches have witnessed the dramatic transformation of thousands of people who were willing to commit themselves to at least a 12-week program. Likewise, countless people have placed their feet solidly on the path to long-term financial fitness by committing to adopt an envelope system and live by the principles outlined in this book. This path may not be easy at times, but it will get easier as you move forward. Financial fitness can be as close as 12 short weeks away!

■ APPLIED PRINCIPLE 18

Maintain and increase financial fitness beyond 12 weeks.

Ryan and Christine Richardson were dedicated to completing the 12-week challenge Tom gave them. During this time, they were successful in transforming their thinking and in addressing their poor financial habits. During these three short months, the envelope system created a new way of thinking and allowed them to start living a new way of life.

Obviously, achieving long-term financial fitness is contingent on your ability to consistently apply the principles you have learned. Successful athletes will tell you that taking off as little as a few weeks from consistent conditioning can be very detrimental to their overall fitness level. So is the case with financial fitness. If you want to create long-term financial fitness, you need to continue applying the principles you have learned. As soon as you stop living within your means, you begin to jeopardize your financial future and the achievement of the goals you have set. Consistently following the five steps outlined below will help you maintain and enhance your long-term financial fitness:

1. After completing your first spending plan, review it and make appropriate adjustments each month. This should always be done with your partner. Make sure you continue to live within your means every month. At the end of each month, transfer the amount you have saved to additional savings, prudent investments, or increased debt reduction.
2. Set aside at least 5 percent of your net monthly income for savings. Consistently increase this amount as you eliminate debt and find other ways to save.
3. After defining your first net-worth statement, update it every 90 days. Review your progress and make appropriate adjustments to your long-term financial goals.
4. After defining your debt-elimination plan, review your progress every 90 days and make sure you are on track with your debt-reduction objectives.
5. As you successfully eliminate debt, transfer the amount you were paying to satisfy debt into savings and sound investments. This added amount will assist you greatly in achieving your long-term financial objectives.

THE PRINCIPLES OF MONEY FOR LIFE

The Lifelong Pursuit of Financial Fitness

What does it mean to be physically fit? For some, being physically fit means having the strength and endurance necessary to win a marathon; for others, it is simply to finish. While some want to be able to compete at a professional level, most agree that being physically fit means having a level of fitness necessary to look good, enjoy a healthy life, and be able to participate comfortably in the activities they like. There is no predefined point at which we suddenly become physically fit. Physical fitness is more about being on the right path and doing the right things from a diet and exercise perspective than reaching some magical point in time. However, having specific and attainable objectives that provide motivation for continual improvement is very important. Otherwise, we may struggle with direction and find it difficult to stay on the right path.

Financial fitness is also more about being on the right path than it is about reaching some magical number on a net-worth statement. Clearly, it is more a state of mind than a specific level of wealth. And like the concept of physical fitness, setting appropriate goals and objectives will provide motivation for continual improvement. Most people know if they need to become more financially fit. This knowledge generally stems from their daily interaction with issues surrounding money. Ryan and Christine found that most other things in their life were taking a backseat because of the constant stress and strain from poor financial health. However, within a few short weeks of changing directions and applying the principles outlined in this book, they found this stress and strain replaced with excitement, relief, and peace. After spending so much time and energy worrying about paying the next bill, running out of money before the end of the month, an increasing debt load, and maxing out their credit cards, they were able to focus attention on the things in life that were most important–including their relationship, their children, and their future.

Perhaps financial fitness can best be measured by how we feel as we interact with money on a daily basis. The following is a list of the many thoughts and feelings that await you as you take the steps to become financially fit:

1. You have money set aside for the holidays before the shopping begins.

2. As you take your next vacation, you know that it is completely paid for before you leave.
3. The next time a major appliance needs to be replaced, you have the money already set aside.
4. You are able to go to work every day knowing that if you lose your job or have a major illness, you have sufficient emergency funds set aside to carry you through.
5. Next year when school starts, you are able to purchase school clothes and supplies from money that is already set aside.
6. You never need to worry about checking the account balance at the bank before you pay a bill.
7. You are excited to get the next credit card statement, because you know that the balance is shrinking and if any purchases have been made, you already have the money set aside to pay for them in full.
8. Picking up the mail every day is not a drudgery, because you know that all of the bills coming in are just part of your spending plan and have been anticipated in advance.
9. You look forward to making decisions regarding the education of your children, because you are actively saving money for this purpose.
10. You spend time planning and anticipating retirement, because you are debt free and prudently investing money to fund the lifestyle you want to have.
11. Financial discussions with your partner are more focused on reviewing progress and planning for the future than on the last credit card statement, late bill, or emotional purchase.
12. You find it appealing to have financial discussions rather than practicing an avoidance strategy and hoping somehow the problems will just magically disappear.
13. The next time you make a major purchase like an automobile or a house, you are more excited about having completed the purchase within the guidelines of your financial plan than about the specific details of what was purchased.
14. The last thought on your mind as you drift off to sleep is about how much fun your upcoming vacation will be rather than a worrisome question of how you will be able to make ends meet.

Being able to have these thoughts and feelings is not contingent on the amount of money you make or your net worth. You do not have to be rich to enjoy this level of financial peace and happiness. Recent studies have shown that happiness is more a function of principles you live by than the amount of money you make. The only question is, Will you take the steps necessary to change direction and start down the path to financial fitness? This book has provided the blueprint necessary to achieve the peace and happiness that is reserved for those who commit to lifelong financial fitness. Specifically, the following 18 principles were addressed:

1. The financial path we should seek is the path least traveled.
2. Awareness is the first step on the path.
3. Sincere desire is the second step on the path.
4. Becoming truly committed is the first obstacle to real change.
5. Be prepared to change your thinking.
6. Take a candid assessment by preparing a net-worth statement.
7. Spend less than you make.
8. Implement the Success Cycle.
9. Learn the secret of envelope budgeting.
10. Create a spending plan.
11. Use an envelope budgeting system to track every expense.
12. Make appropriate spending decisions.
13. Review your plan at least monthly.
14. Repeat the Success Cycle each month.
15. Use an envelope system to rapidly eliminate debt.
16. Use credit cards appropriately.
17. Make a 12-week commitment.
18. Maintain and increase financial fitness beyond 12 weeks.

The financial position you are in today will not be the financial position you are in tomorrow–it will be either better or worse. Change is inevitable. You cannot stop change from taking place; you can only determine the direction it will take. You know better than anyone else the rewards associated with the way you currently interact with money. Achieving long-term financial fitness takes courage, discipline, sacrifice, and consistent effort, but the rewards can be extraordinary. What direction will you choose?

Epilogue
One year later . . .

RYAN AND CHRISTINE RICHARDSON

Ryan and Christine have substantially reduced their consumer debt. They have completely paid off their store charge card and both of their credit cards, and they are seven months away from paying off their auto loan. Since they no longer need two credit cards, they've eliminated one. They now only use one card, have enough money allocated through their credit card repayment envelope each month to cover whatever they charge, and because of the accelerator created by the elimination of other debt, they are paying down their remaining debt at an ever-increasing rate. In one year, they will have eliminated all of their debt, with the exception of their mortgage.

Ryan received higher-than-average bonuses over the past year and received another substantial raise. Christine also received a good raise at her school. Instead of automatically spending more because of their increased income, they took a careful look at all of their spending accounts and revised their current plan to put more into debt payments and savings, with some necessary increases to a few key spending accounts. They are on pace to eliminate all of their debt within about seven years. With the extra income and the money they've freed up by eliminating debt, they are not only increasing the rate at which they can pay off their remaining debt, they have begun to invest some of their money for college and retirement. They plan to meet with Tom Maxwell again in another year to go over a thorough financial plan for their future. Ryan and Christine no longer bicker about money and are able to discuss financial issues freely and naturally.

■ ROB AND SUSAN GOLDMAN

Rob and Susan met with Tom Maxwell, who challenged them to use the same principles that Ryan and Christine had put to work. Going through the initial setup phase of the process was an eye-opener for Susan. At first, it was difficult for Susan to get used to paying attention to her spending in this way, but she could see the positive results her change in behavior was having and stuck with it. Rob, who was surprised himself to discover how much he was spending in certain categories each month, learned more than he realized he would. Although they've only been using an envelope system for nine months, they have worked with Tom to create a plan to substantially reduce their debt at an accelerated pace, and to create a college fund for Megan that will be the primary focus of their savings before creating a separate retirement account for themselves and another college fund for Danny. Although it hasn't always been easy, both Rob and Susan have found the use of the envelope principles to be far easier than going down the road they had been on a year before.

■ SHIRLEY CHANG

Shirley saw her son David enter high school in the fall. She is currently on track to completely eliminate her debt within three years and has a substantial amount of money put away for David's—and Sam's—college tuition. Now, when Shirley goes shopping with Christine, they compare notes on how well each is doing that month staying on top of their spending accounts.

■ JOHN AND PATTY RICHARDSON

Following her conversation with Ryan in the kitchen after the barbeque last year, Patty decided to have a talk with her husband John after all. Although John was reluctant to discuss it, they did eventually come to an agreement that something needed to be done differently. When Ryan told his father about meeting Walter and Lucy Howard, and how much they had accumulated over the years, John decided to work with

Patty on an envelope budgeting system. After creating a new spending plan with the help of their financial advisor, both John and Patty decided to put off retirement for another year, so that they could eliminate more of their debt while they were still bringing in more income. Now, both John and Patty are looking forward to retirement, secure in the knowledge that they have more control over their money.

■ WALTER AND LUCY HOWARD

Walter and Lucy returned from their cruise in Scandinavia in July and, a month later, visited their daughter's family in Boston. Walter sold the fast-food franchise for a substantial amount in the fall. He and Lucy made the first of nine planned $10,000 gifts, this first one to their oldest grandchild, Anthony, who will be enrolling in Stanford University next fall. The money will help pay for tuition, books, and room and board.

Afterword

I hope you enjoyed reading *Money for Life.* I felt a strong motivation to write it. I am certain that when the principles outlined in this book are followed, you will achieve the same satisfaction and financial success that the Richardsons experienced. I know this from personal experience. This is one of the primary reasons I assisted with developing Mvelopes® Personal, a computer-based envelope spending management system.

My challenge to you is to try these principles for yourself. The simple truth is, it is impossible to get out of debt or build wealth if you spend more per month than you make. This seems obvious, but many people continue to overspend. And the primary reason is ineffective spending management. Everyone needs a spending plan regardless of how much they make. Whether you use cash, paper and pencil, a spreadsheet, Mvelopes Personal, or something else, you need to do something. And you need to get started now–it's that important. It will not only affect your long-term financial security, but also your happiness–believe me!

Fortunately, you don't need to rely on my word alone. With the software on the enclosed CD, you will be able to use the Mvelopes Personal system free of charge for 30 days. If you consistently apply the principles outlined in this book and continue using Mvelopes Personal, you will significantly enhance your long-term financial security, as Ryan and Christine Richardson did, and as thousands of their real-life counterparts have.

Thank you for reading *Money for Life.* I wish you success in taking your next step toward financial fitness.

Steven B. Smith

Notes

1. Page xv. *Total consumer debt in the United States exceeds $1.8 trillion:* Federal Reserve statistical release, "Consumer Credit, September 2003," 7 November 2003.

2. Page xv. *Average household debt as a percentage of annual net income:* Dave Anderton, "Pulling out the plastic," *Salt Lake City Deseret News,* 8 December 2002.

3. Page xv. *Increase in those seeking protection from creditors through personal bankruptcy is growing:* Jay Evensen, "Consumer plagued by credit that is too easy," *Salt Lake City Deseret News,* 8 December 2002.

4. Page xv. *Financial issues remain a significant cause of contention in homes:* "Marriage Report–The Truth about Women, Men, and Money," *Redbook,* November 2003, p. 102.

5. Page xv. *Financial issues at home are one of the greatest contributors to divorce:* James P. Christensen, Clint Combs, and George D. Durrant, *Rich on Any Income* (Salt Lake City: Shadow Mountain, 1985).

6. Page 19. *The average American family carries credit card debt of more than $6,500:* Federal Reserve statistical release, "Consumer Credit, September 2003," 7 November 2003.

7. Page 19. *20 percent of respondents said they were carrying a credit card balance of over $10,000:* "Marriage Report–The Truth about Women, Men, and Money," *Redbook,* November 2003, p. 106.

8. Page 19. *More than 75 percent of graduating college seniors in America have credit card debt:* Dave Ramsey, *The Total Money Makeover* (Nashville, Tenn.: Thomas Nelson, 2003).

9. Page 19. *70 percent of Americans live paycheck to paycheck:* Dave Ramsey, *The Total Money Makeover* (Nashville, Tenn.: Thomas Nelson, 2003).

10. Page 34. *Total consumer debt in the United States exceeds $1.8 trillion, average consumer debt per household exceeds $17,000, average credit card debt per household exceeds $6,500:* Federal Reserve statistical release, "Consumer Credit, September 2003," 7 November 2003.

11. Page 34. *The average American has nine credit cards:* Jay Evensen, "Consumer plagued by credit that is too easy," *Salt Lake City Deseret News,* 8 December 2002.

12. Page 34. *70 percent of Americans live paycheck to paycheck:* Dave Ramsey, *The Total Money Makeover* (Nashville, Tenn.: Thomas Nelson, 2003).

13. Page 35. *The average equity in our homes has actually declined:* Federal Reserve Board, "Mortgage Refinancing in 2001 and Early 2002," prepared for the Division of Research and Statistics by Glenn Canner, Karen Dynan, and Wayne Passmore, December 2002.

14. Page 36. *People who become wealthy live well below their incomes:* Thomas J. Stanley, Ph.D., and William D. Danko, Ph.D., *The Millionaire Next Door* (New York: Pocket Books, 1998).

15. Page 41. *Tests have shown that on average, individuals will spend 10 to 12 percent more for the same items and services with plastic than they will with cash:* http://www.cardweb.com.

16. Page 42. *As a society, we do a very poor job of providing even basic personal financial management training:* Federal Reserve Board, "Financial Literacy: An Overview of Practice, Research, and Policy," prepared for the Division of Consumer and Community Affairs by Sandra Braunstein and Carolyn Welch, November 2002.

17. Page 42. *Companies provide easy access to consumer credit:* Federal Reserve Board, "Recent Changes in U.S. Family Finances: Evidence from the 1998 and 2001 Survey of Consumer Finances," prepared for the Division of Research and Statistics by Ana M. Aizcorbe, Arthur B. Kennickell, and Devin B. Moore, January 2003.

18. Page 44. *Why are so many people interested in what we have to say?:* Thomas J. Stanley, Ph.D., and William D. Danko, Ph.D., *The Millionaire Next Door* (New York: Pocket Books, 1998).

19. Page 52. *Some years ago, Frank Burge told a story regarding management styles:* Frank Burge, "Fire-hose management. And a better way," *Electronic Business,* 7 October 1991, p. 195.

20. Page 89. *There are more than three billion credit card offers mailed out each year:* Jay Evensen, "Consumer plagued by credit that is too easy," *Salt Lake City Deseret News,* 8 December 2002.

21. Page 90. *Collective debt of Americans now totals nearly 110 percent of total annual net income:* Dave Anderton, "Pulling out the plastic," *Salt Lake City Deseret News,* 8 December 2002.

22. Page 130. *Only about one-third of those with credit cards pay their balance in full each month:* http://www.cardweb.com.

23. Page 130. *The interest rate associated with the outstanding balance on credit card accounts generally averages about 12 percent:* Federal Reserve statistical release, "Consumer Credit, September 2003," 7 November 2003.

24. Page 136. *Studies have shown that happiness is more a function of principles you live by than the amount of money you make:* Jean Chatzky, *You Don't Have to be Rich* (New York: Penguin, 2003).

Appendix A ■ Twelve-Week Checklist

Ryan and Christine experienced a personal financial transformation by accepting a 12-week challenge from Tom and committing to following the principles outlined in this book. You can experience your own financial transformation by following the steps outlined in the 12-week checklist.

■ INITIAL PREPARATION

____ Make a commitment (with your partner, if applicable) to change your financial direction and become financially fit. (See Applied Principle 4, page 24, and the Principles of Money for Life, page 134.)

____ Write down a list of financial objectives—things in your financial life that you would most like to change. (See Applied Principle 4 and the Principles of Money for Life.)

____ Write down a list of the obstacles that may stand in your way—things that have knocked you off course in the past. (See step 2 of Applied Principle 4, page 25.)

____ Make a commitment to complete the 12-week program. (See Applied Principle 5, page 27, and Applied Principle 17, page 132.)

____ Prepare a net-worth statement. (See Applied Principle 6, page 44.)

____ Make a commitment (with your partner, if applicable) to spend less than you make. (See Applied Principle 7, page 50.)

____ Review and understand the steps of the Success Cycle. (See Applied Principle 8, page 52.)

____ Review and understand the principles of the envelope budgeting system. (See Applied Principle 9, page 69.)

____ Select an envelope budgeting tool. (See Applied Principle 9, Appendix B, page 155, and Appendix E, page 179.)

■ WEEK 1 Plan and Track

____ Create a balanced monthly spending plan. (See Applied Principle 10, page 75, and Appendix C, page 167.)

____ Create the beginning balances for your spending accounts, or envelopes. (See step 4 of Appendix B, pages 157 and 161, and Appendix E, page 179.)

____ Allocate your monthly deposits to your spending accounts. (See step 2 of Appendix B, page 156, and Appendix E.)

____ Using your selected envelope tool, track all transactions for the week. If you are using Mvelopes® Personal, download and assign all transactions at least three times during the week. (See Applied Principle 11, page 105, step 5 of Appendix B, pages 158 and 161, and Appendix E.)

____ With the help of your selected envelope tool, make appropriate spending decisions by spending from the balance remaining in each spending account. (See steps 2 and 3 of Applied Principle 9, page 72, Applied Principle 12, page 107, Appendix B, and Appendix E.)

____ Make any envelope-to-envelope transfers that you believe are appropriate. (See step 3 of Applied Principle 9, page 72, Applied Principle 13, page 109, Appendix B, and Appendix E.)

■ WEEK 2 Track

____ Allocate your monthly deposits to your spending accounts. (See Week 1.)

____ Track all transactions for the week. (See Week 1.)

____ Make appropriate spending decisions by spending from the balance remaining in each spending account. (See Week 1.)

____ Make any envelope-to-envelope transfers that you believe are appropriate. (See Week 1.)

■ WEEK 3 Track

____ Allocate your monthly deposits to your spending accounts. (See Week 1.)

____ Track all transactions for the week. (See Week 1.)

____ Make appropriate spending decisions by spending from the balance remaining in each spending account. (See Week 1.)

____ Make any envelope-to-envelope transfers that you believe are appropriate. (See Week 1.)

■ WEEK 4 Track

____ Allocate your monthly deposits to your spending accounts. (See Week 1.)

____ Track all transactions for the week. (See Week 1.)

____ Make appropriate spending decisions by spending from the balance remaining in each spending account. (See Week 1.)

____ Make any envelope-to-envelope transfers that you believe are appropriate. (See Week 1.)

■ WEEK 5 Compare, Adjust, Plan, and Track

____ Using your selected envelope tool, create a report showing the total amount spent and the amount remaining in each spending account. (See Applied Principle 13, page 109, step 6 of Appendix B, page 159, and Appendix E, page 179.)

____ Compare actual spending to planned spending for each spending account. (See Applied Principle 13, Appendix B, and Appendix E.)

____ Make appropriate adjustments, including envelope-to-envelope transfers and monthly income allocation amounts, and set beginning balances for next month's plan. (See Applied Principle 13, Applied Principle 14, page 115, Appendix B, and Appendix E.)

____ Prepare your debt roll-down schedule and make sure you have created the correct debt payment accounts, with their corresponding income allocations. (See Applied Principle 15, page 116, Appendix E, page 184, and Appendix D, page 175.)

____ Allocate your monthly deposits to your spending accounts. (See Week 1.)

____ Track all transactions for the week. (See Week 1.)

____ Make appropriate spending decisions by spending from the balance remaining in each spending account. (See Week 1.)

____ Make any envelope-to-envelope transfers that you believe are appropriate. (See Week 1.)

WEEKS 6 THROUGH 8 Track

____ Allocate your monthly deposits to your spending accounts weekly. (See Week 1.)

____ Track all transactions for each week. (See Week 1.)

____ Make appropriate spending decisions by spending from the balance remaining in each spending account. (See Week 1.)

____ Make any envelope-to-envelope transfers that you believe are appropriate. (See Week 1.)

WEEK 9 Compare, Adjust, Plan, and Track

____ Create a report showing the total amount spent and the amount remaining in each spending account. (See Week 5.)

____ Compare actual spending to planned spending for each spending account. (See Week 5.)

____ Make appropriate adjustments, including envelope-to-envelope transfers and monthly income allocation amounts, and set beginning balances for next month's plan. (See Week 5.)

____ Review your debt elimination plan and make appropriate adjustments. (See Week 5.)

____ Allocate your monthly deposits to your spending accounts. (See Week 1.)

____ Track all transactions for the week. (See Week 1.)

____ Make appropriate spending decisions by spending from the balance remaining in each spending account. (See Week 1.)

____ Make any envelope-to-envelope transfers that you believe are appropriate. (See Week 1.)

WEEKS 10 THROUGH 12 Track

____ Allocate your monthly deposits to your spending accounts each week. (See Week 1.)

____ Track all transactions for each week. (See Week 1.)

____ Make appropriate spending decisions by spending from the balance remaining in each spending account. (See Week 1.)

____ Make any envelope-to-envelope transfers that you believe are appropriate. (See Week 1.)

TWELVE-WEEK WRAP-UP

____ Create a report showing the total amount spent and the amount remaining in each spending account. (See Week 5.)

____ Compare actual spending to planned spending for each spending account. (See Week 5.)

____ Make appropriate adjustments, including envelope-to-envelope transfers and monthly income allocation amounts, and set beginning balances for next month's plan. (See Week 5.)

____ Update your net-worth statement. (See Applied Principle 6, page 44.)

____ Review your personal financial objectives and make necessary adjustments. (See Applied Principle 4, page 24 and the Principles of Money for Life, page 134.)

____ Make a commitment (with your partner, if applicable) to maintain and increase financial fitness beyond 12 weeks. (See Applied Principle 18, page 133, and the Principles of Money for Life.)

Appendix B ■ Choosing an Envelope Budgeting System

There are many ways to successfully implement and apply the envelope principles discussed in detail in this book. However, finding the right tool is important to ensure your long-term success. The correct implementation tool must assist you in successfully tracking all expenses and maintaining the balance information that is necessary to make informed spending decisions on a daily basis.

As was discussed previously, there are four basic approaches to an implementation of the envelope principles: (1) cash, (2) a paper ledger or computer spreadsheet, (3) a computer-based envelope system, or (4) a combination of these. Choosing the correct implementation tool is a matter of personal preference and lifestyle. Because selecting the best approach is an important part of successful implementation, each approach will be discussed in greater detail below.

■ CASH-BASED ENVELOPES

The most basic approach to implementing the envelope principles is using a cash system. Income allocation and spending tracking are very straightforward with cash. Because of these advantages, many people have opted to use the cash system. However, because it is more difficult and inconvenient to make all payments with cash, many people combine a cash-based envelope system with a system that can handle the management of non-cash transactions. This section will focus on a complete cash approach to provide an overview of how this system functions.

FIGURE B.1 ■ Monthly Net Income

Monthly Net Income

Income Source	Payment #	Amount	Date
ABC Corporation	Check # 1	$1,200.00	7th
	Check # 2	$1,200.00	21st
XYZ Company	Check # 1	$2,000.00	10th
Total Net Income		$4,400.00	

STEP 1: Create a monthly spending plan.

Whether you use a cash-based system or any other system, the first step is always to define a monthly spending plan (see Applied Principle 10, page 75). Remember, this is the process of defining your monthly net income and creating spending accounts, or envelopes. With the cash-based system, you should first create this monthly plan on paper so you have a road map to follow. On the top of a blank sheet of paper, define your monthly net income. Under each source of income, identify the individual checks you will receive this month. Make sure to include the amount of each check and the date you will receive it. (See Figure B.1.)

Next, write down a list of the envelope spending accounts you want to utilize (see step 2 of Applied Principle 10, page 79). After you have completed your list, write the amount of money you will place into each envelope this month next to each spending account name. (See Figure B.2.)

STEP 2: Create a monthly income allocation plan.

When you have completed this, you need to plan how you will fund each envelope. To do this, create a new column for each check you will receive during the month. Include the amount of the check beneath the column header. Then, determine the amount of money from each check

FIGURE B.2 ■ Envelope Spending Accounts

Envelope Spending Accounts

Envelope Spending Accounts	Monthly Allocation Amounts	Envelope Spending Accounts	Monthly Allocation Amounts
Monthly Required		**Periodic Required**	
Mortgage	$1,250	Auto Registration	$20
Auto Loan	$375	Property Tax	$100
Credit Card #1	$150	Homeowner's Insurance	$75
Credit Card #2	$75	Life Insurance	$40
Savings	$200	**Subtotal**	**$235**
Auto Insurance	$120		
Power	$75		
Natural Gas	$65		
Water/Sewer/Garbage	$35		
Day Care	$275		
Subtotal	**$2,630**		
Monthly Discretionary		**Periodic Discretionary**	
Auto Fuel	$175	Medical Deductible	$55
Babysitter	$25	Birthday Gifts	$25
Clothing	$150	Holiday Gifts	$70
Entertainment	$75	Auto Maintenance	$40
Eating Out	$50	House Maintenance	$40
Groceries	$325	Vacation	$150
His Spending	$50	Donations	$125
Her Spending	$50	**Subtotal**	**$505**
Phone- House	$75		
Phone- Mobile	$65		
Subtotal	**$1,040**	Total Monthly Required	$2,630
		Total Monthly Discretionary	$1,040
		Total Periodic Required	$235
		Total Periodic Discretionary	$505
		Total Monthly Allocations*	**$4,400**

*Total Monthly Allocations = Total Net Income

that you will place into each envelope. You should prioritize these income allocations based on which payments will need to be made first during the month. Make sure you allocate each check completely. (See Figure B.3.)

STEP 3: Set up your envelopes.

Next, you will want to create your actual envelopes. This can be done using standard envelopes or any other type of organizing system you prefer. You only need to make sure each envelope is properly labeled.

STEP 4: Allocate your cash on hand.

Once this is completed, you will need to determine how you will allocate any money you currently have on hand. For example, if you have $500 on hand, determine into which envelopes you will place this money.

FIGURE B.3 ■ Income Allocation Plan

Income Allocation Plan

Envelope Spending Accounts	Monthly Allocation Amounts	Monthly Income 7th Income #1 Check #1 $1,200	10th Income #2 Check #1 $2,000	21st Income #1 Check #2 $1,200
Monthly Required				
Mortgage	$1,250	$1,200	$50	
Auto Loan	$375		$375	
Credit Card #1	$150		$150	
Credit Card #2	$75		$75	
Savings	$200		$200	
Auto Insurance	$120		$120	
Power	$75		$75	
Natural Gas	$65		$65	
Water/Sewer/Garbage	$35		$35	
Day Care	$275		$275	
Subtotal	**$2,630**			
Monthly Discretionary				
Auto Fuel	$175		$175	
Babysitter	$25		$25	
Clothing	$150		$150	
Entertainment	$75		$75	
Eating Out	$50		$50	
Groceries	$325		$105	$220
His Spending	$50			$50
Her Spending	$50			$50
Phone- House	$75			$75
Phone- Mobile	$65			$65
Subtotal	**$1,040**			
Periodic Required				
Auto Registration	$20			$20
Property Tax	$100			$100
Homeowner's Insurance	$75			$75
Life Insurance	$40			$40
Subtotal	**$235**			
Periodic Discretionary				
Medical Deductible	$55			$55
Birthday Gifts	$25			$25
Holiday Gifts	$70			$70
Auto Maintenance	$40			$40
House Maintenance	$40			$40
Vacation	$150			$150
Donations	$125			$125
Subtotal	**$505**			
Total Monthly Allocations*	**$4,400**	**$1,200**	**$2,000**	**$1,200**

*Total Monthly Allocations = Total Net Income

STEP 5: Allocate income and track expenses.

After you have completed this step, you are prepared to begin the funding and tracking process. As you receive each check, follow the funding plan you have devised. As you make a purchase or pay a bill, use the cash resources from the envelope set aside for that purpose. If you transfer money from one envelope to another, indicate the date and the amount of the transfer on each envelope so that you are able to track the actual amount allocated to an envelope during the month. This information may be needed to make proper adjustments at the end of the month.

STEP 6: Complete a monthly review and create next month's plan.

Once you have completed the first month, you can begin your monthly review (see Applied Principle 13, page 109). As you complete this review, you will prepare your spending plan for the following month. Remember, there may be some months when you will receive periodic income like commissions and bonuses. For the months you receive these checks, you will need to include them in your funding plan for the month (see Appendix C, page 167, for a summary of how to successfully handle variable income). If you receive your paycheck every other week, there will be two months in the year when you will receive three checks. During these months, you will need to determine how you would like to allocate this income.

■ PAPER LEDGER OR COMPUTER SPREADSHEETS

Using a paper ledger or computer spreadsheet system allows you to track all types of spending. This approach works much the same way as the cash-based envelope system, with a few adjustments. Obviously, you will not be allocating actual cash to spending envelopes. However, you will be creating spending accounts that are essentially virtual envelopes. Your cash will stay in your bank account, but you will allocate it to many spending accounts for the purpose of tracking your spending and determining the balance remaining in each spending account on a daily basis. A combination of systems can be used, but this section will focus on the paper ledger or spreadsheet approach.

STEP 1: Create a monthly spending plan.

Follow Step 1 as outlined in the cash-based section on page 156.

STEP 2: Create a monthly income allocation plan.

Follow Step 2 as outlined in the cash-based section on page 156.

STEP 3: Set up your envelopes.

With the cash-based system, you create actual envelopes as spending accounts. Then as you receive cash, you divide the cash between the envelopes as outlined on your funding and allocation plan. When you are using a paper ledger or computer spreadsheet system, you will need to create a separate ledger account for each spending account. The beginning balance for each of these accounts should be placed at zero. (See Figure B.4.)

FIGURE B.4 ■ Spending Account Ledger

Spending Account Ledger

Spending Account: Groceries

Date	ID #	Description	Deposit +	Expense -	Balance
1-Feb	n/a	Beginning Balance			0.00

STEP 4: Allocate your cash on hand.

With the cash-based system, your cash on hand will be allocated completely to your envelopes. With a paper ledger or computer spreadsheet system, your cash will be in a bank account or accounts. You can use any number of bank accounts with the ledger or spreadsheet system; however, it is easier to track if you do all of your spending from one bank account. With the ledger or spreadsheet approach, the amount of money you have in your bank account or accounts should be equal to the combined total of each of your spending accounts. Normally, when you begin using an envelope budgeting system, you will have some cash in your account. You will need to determine the amount of money in your bank account and allocate this amount to your spending accounts. When you are finished with this step, your system should be balanced. (See Figure B.5.)

STEP 5: Allocate income and track expenses.

You are now ready to begin using your ledger or spreadsheet system. Each time you receive a deposit in your bank account, you will need to allocate this money to your spending accounts. Do this by following the funding plan you created in Step 2. The total amount of the deposit should equal the combined amount of money deposited in each of your spending accounts. (See Figure B.6.)

Each time you make a purchase or pay a bill, record the transaction on your bank account ledger and on the appropriate spending account ledger. It is usually best to record the transaction identifier–that is, check number, if there is one–on each ledger. Sometimes you will make a payment for goods or services that relates to two or more spending accounts. An example of this would be purchasing food and an article of clothing in the same transaction. In this case, you will need to record the total transaction amount on your bank account ledger and then split the transaction appropriately between your grocery and clothing accounts. If you use a credit card, you will need to follow the recommendations found in Applied Principle 16, page 130. (See Figure B.7.)

Remember, all miscellaneous transactions that come through your bank account also must be subtracted from an appropriate spending account. An example of a miscellaneous charge would be a bank fee.

FIGURE B.5 ■ Beginning Balances for Spending Accounts

Beginning Balances for Spending Accounts

Envelope Spending Accounts	Balance
Monthly Required	
Mortgage	$50
Auto Loan	$200
Credit Card #1	$0
Credit Card #2	$0
Savings	$0
Auto Insurance	$0
Power	$75
Natural Gas	$0
Water/Sewer/Garbage	$0
Day Care	$0
Monthly Discretionary	
Auto Fuel	$50
Babysitter	$0
Clothing	$0
Entertainment	$25
Eating Out	$0
Groceries	$100
His Spending	$0
Her Spending	$0
Phone- House	$0
Phone- Mobile	$0
Periodic Required	
Auto Registration	$0
Property Tax	$0
Homeowner's Insurance	$0
Life Insurance	$0
Periodic Discretionary	
Medical Deductible	$0
Birthday Gifts	$0
Holiday Gifts	$0
Auto Maintenance	$0
House Maintenance	$0
Vacation	$0
Donations	$0
Balance Allocated to Spending Accounts	$500
Total Actual Cash On Hand 1-Feb	$500
Difference	$0

FIGURE B.6 ■ Allocating Deposits

Allocating Deposits

Spending Account: Groceries

Date	ID #	Description	Deposit +	Expense -	Balance
1-Feb	n/a	Beginning Balance			$ -
1-Feb	n/a	Allocation of Cash on Hand	$ 100.00		$ 100.00
10-Feb	n/a	February Allocation (XYZ)	$ 220.00		$ 320.00
21-Feb	n/a	February Allocation (ABC)	$ 105.00		$ 425.00

FIGURE B.7 ■ Expense Tracking

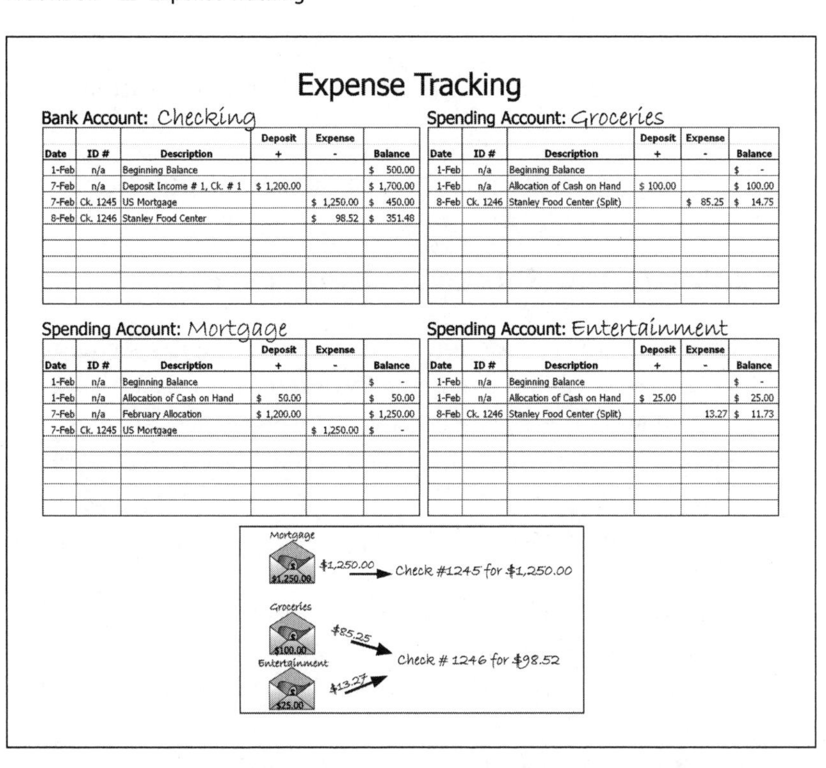

Expense Tracking

Bank Account: Checking

Date	ID #	Description	Deposit +	Expense -	Balance
1-Feb	n/a	Beginning Balance			$ 500.00
7-Feb	n/a	Deposit Income # 1, Ck. # 1	$ 1,200.00		$ 1,700.00
7-Feb	Ck. 1245	US Mortgage		$ 1,250.00	$ 450.00
8-Feb	Ck. 1246	Stanley Food Center		$ 98.52	$ 351.48

Spending Account: Groceries

Date	ID #	Description	Deposit +	Expense -	Balance
1-Feb	n/a	Beginning Balance			$ -
1-Feb	n/a	Allocation of Cash on Hand	$ 100.00		$ 100.00
8-Feb	Ck. 1246	Stanley Food Center (Split)		$ 85.25	$ 14.75

Spending Account: Mortgage

Date	ID #	Description	Deposit +	Expense -	Balance
1-Feb	n/a	Beginning Balance			$ -
1-Feb	n/a	Allocation of Cash on Hand	$ 50.00		$ 50.00
7-Feb	n/a	February Allocation	$ 1,200.00		$ 1,250.00
7-Feb	Ck. 1245	US Mortgage		$ 1,250.00	$ -

Spending Account: Entertainment

Date	ID #	Description	Deposit +	Expense -	Balance
1-Feb	n/a	Beginning Balance			$ -
1-Feb	n/a	Allocation of Cash on Hand	$ 25.00		$ 25.00
8-Feb	Ck. 1246	Stanley Food Center (Split)		13.27	$ 11.73

FIGURE B.8 Spending Account Transfer

Spending Account Transfer

Spending Account: Savings

Date	ID #	Description	Deposit +	Expense -	Balance
1-Feb	n/a	Beginning Balance			$ -
10-Feb	n/a	February Allocation	$ 200.00		$ 200.00
1-Mar	n/a	Transfer from Groceries	$ 24.12		$ 224.12

Spending Account: Groceries

Date	ID #	Description	Deposit +	Expense -	Balance
1-Feb	n/a	Beginning Balance			$ -
1-Feb	n/a	Allocation of Cash on Hand	$ 100.00		$ 100.00
8-Feb	Ck 1246	Stanley Food Center (Split)		$ 85.25	$ 14.75
25-Feb	n/a	February Allocation		$ 325.00	$ 339.75
27-Feb	Ck. 1265	Stanley Food Center		$ 215.63	$ 124.12
1-Mar	n/a	Transfer to Savings		$ 24.12	$ 100.00

Finally, if you need to transfer money from one spending account to another (i.e., an envelope-to-envelope transfer), you should indicate the transfer on each of the appropriate spending account ledgers. (See Figure B.8.)

STEP 6: Complete a monthly review and create next month's plan.

Follow Step 6 as outlined in the cash-based section on page 159.

■ COMPUTER-BASED ENVELOPE SYSTEM

Perhaps the easiest envelope system for most to use is computer based. A computer-based system allows you to follow each of the six steps outlined above for the cash, ledger, or spreadsheet systems. The right system will help you complete each of the following:

1. Create your monthly spending plan.
2. Set up your spending accounts.
3. Create your funding, or income allocation, plan.
4. Set your initial spending account balances.
5. Ensure your spending accounts and bank accounts are balanced.
6. Allocate your income to spending accounts as defined in your funding plan.

7. Automatically track your transactions.
8. Assign your transactions to the appropriate spending accounts.
9. Split transactions between a number of spending accounts.
10. Set aside money for credit card purchases.
11. Complete a monthly review and make adjustments.

An appropriate computer-based system also will generate a number of important reports, including spending and bank account summary reports. These reports can be printed on a daily basis and carried with you to assist with making sound spending decisions. It also should help facilitate the monthly reconciliation process for your financial institution accounts.

The tool that Tom introduced Ryan and Christine to was Mvelopes® Personal, a computer-based envelope system that connects to the Internet to automatically track all of their transactions. For more details on this system, refer to Appendix E, page 179.

■ USING A COMBINATION OF APPROACHES

Even if you use a paper ledger system, computer spreadsheet, or computer-based envelope system, there may be certain spending accounts for which you would like to use cash. This is not a problem and can easily be done. Most people who use a combined approach use cash envelopes for many of their monthly discretionary accounts, such as groceries, entertainment, allowances, and clothing. They find they are able to exact a higher level of control over these spending areas when they are using cash.

If you would like to use cash for some of your spending accounts, you will need to go to the bank or ATM once each month and take out enough cash to meet the funding, or income allocation, requirements for these envelopes.

Appendix C

Using Variable Income with an Envelope Budgeting System

Variable income sources include commissions, bonuses, and other types of income that may vary in amount and frequency. Most real estate agents, for example, have completely variable income–they do not receive a paycheck until they have sold a property. When a property is sold, their paycheck is in the form of a commission and is tied to the purchase price of the property. Income is 100 percent variable for many types of employment.

Some types of employment have a fixed-income component and a variable-income component. An example of this may be a sales representative who receives a portion of income in fixed salary and a variable commission based on sales achievement.

For other types of employment, only a small portion of annual income is variable pay. Examples of this would be those who receive a set salary but also receive a quarterly or annual bonus. This was the case for Ryan. If this is the situation for you, refer to Applied Principle 10, page 75. If the majority of your income is variable in nature, use the information below to successfully implement the envelope system.

Many people struggle with variable income, because it is more difficult to forecast and, therefore, more difficult to make appropriate spending decisions. Those whose income is primarily variable often lament that budgeting is impossible, because they never know exactly when or how much they will be paid. For these people, it is even more important to establish a successful budgeting system, because they need to appropriately allocate their income when they do receive it.

There are many different approaches to successfully planning and managing variable income. Often, these different approaches are tailored to personal preference and circumstance. As finding success with

FIGURE C.1 ■ Defining Variable Income—Fixed Period, Variable Amount

Defining Variable Income
Fixed Period, Variable Amount

Variable Income Source	Pay Period	Net Amount Of Check
ABC Corporation	January	$ 4,100
	February	$ 4,300
	March	$ 4,800
	April	$ 4,200
	May	$ 4,200
	June	$ 4,100
	July	$ 4,800
	August	$ 4,300
	September	$ 4,700
	October	$ 4,300
	November	$ 4,400
	December	$ 4,600
Total Annual Net Income		$ 52,800
Average Monthly Net Income		$ 4,400
Lowest Check Amount		$ 4,100

variable income is very important for many people, the following sections will address a few of the different approaches that can be implemented to achieve financial fitness.

There are generally two types of variable income streams: (1) income streams that are paid at a fixed time but are variable in amount and (2) income streams that are variable in both time and amount. Let's look at some alternatives for addressing each of these.

Income that is received at a designated time but is variable in amount is quite common. An example of this would be a monthly sales commission. If the amount of the commission does not vary widely, you can use a conservative approach to forecast the amount you will receive each month. Look at the last several months and calculate the average amount received. Then use this amount to create your monthly spending plan. You also can choose the check with the lowest amount and use this amount to create your monthly spending plan. (See Figure C.1.)

If you are able to balance your monthly spending plan on this amount of income, then when you receive a higher amount of income in any given month, you can use the additional amount to increase your debt repayment or savings. If you are unable to fund all of your spending accounts on the amount you have selected for your monthly spending plan, and you think it will be difficult to reduce spending in other areas, you can allocate your income in this order:

1. Monthly required spending accounts
2. Monthly discretionary spending accounts
3. Periodic required spending accounts
4. Periodic discretionary spending accounts

When you receive more income than the minimum monthly amount you have decided to use for planning purposes, you can first use this amount to fund the spending accounts that you have been unable to fund to date. Most often, this will be periodic discretionary spending accounts like vacations and holiday gift purchasing. After these accounts have been fully funded per your spending plan, you can allocate any remaining amounts of income to debt repayment and additional savings. (See Figure C.2.)

If the amount you receive each pay period varies widely, you should estimate the amount you will be paid on an annual basis. Try to be conservative with this number, as it's much better to underestimate the amount of income you will receive each year than to overspend. Once you have determined this number, divide it by 12 to determine the average amount you will receive on a monthly basis. Then use this number to create your monthly spending plan. (See Figure C.3.)

As you receive your income, you will want to allocate it according to the previous priority schedule, starting with monthly required spending accounts and ending with periodic discretionary accounts. Once all accounts are fully funded to date, you can place any remaining income in savings. This savings should be treated as an income-holding account. During the months when you receive smaller amounts, you will need to use money from your income-holding account to fund your spending accounts. Unless your variable income decreases dramatically over the period of a year, you will be able to successfully navigate the ups and downs by using this planning strategy. This is also the approach you should use for income streams that vary in both amount and frequency. (See Figure C.4.)

The important thing is to make sure you do not spend more than you have planned in each of your spending accounts. The biggest problems with variable income result from people making spending deci-

FIGURE C.2 ■ Defining Variable Income—Fixed Period, Variable Amount

Allocating Variable Income
Fixed Period, Variable Amount

Envelope Spending Accounts	Monthly Allocation Amount	January Allocations $4,100	Amount Underfunded	February Funding Requirements	February Allocations $4,300	Amount Underfunded	March Funding Requirements	March Allocations $4,800
Monthly Required								
Savings	$ 200	$ 200	$ -	$ 200	$ 200	$ -	$ 200	$ 200
Mortgage	$ 1,250	$ 1,250	$ -	$ 1,250	$ 1,250	$ -	$ 1,250	$ 1,250
Auto Loan	$ 375	$ 375	$ -	$ 375	$ 375	$ -	$ 375	$ 375
Credit Card # 1	$ 150	$ 150	$ -	$ 150	$ 150	$ -	$ 150	$ 150
Credit Card # 2	$ 75	$ 75	$ -	$ 75	$ 75	$ -	$ 75	$ 75
Auto Insurance	$ 120	$ 120	$ -	$ 120	$ 120	$ -	$ 120	$ 120
Power	$ 75	$ 75	$ -	$ 75	$ 75	$ -	$ 75	$ 75
Natural Gas	$ 65	$ 65	$ -	$ 65	$ 65	$ -	$ 65	$ 65
Water/Sewer/Garbage	$ 35	$ 35	$ -	$ 35	$ 35	$ -	$ 35	$ 35
Donations	$ 125	$ 125	$ -	$ 125	$ 125	$ -	$ 125	$ 125
Day Care	$ 275	$ 275	$ -	$ 275	$ 275	$ -	$ 275	$ 275
Subtotal	$ 2,745							
Monthly Discretionary								
Auto Fuel	$ 175	$ 175	$ -	$ 175	$ 175	$ -	$ 175	$ 175
Babysitter	$ 25	$ 25	$ -	$ 25	$ 25	$ -	$ 25	$ 25
Clothing	$ 150	$ 150	$ -	$ 150	$ 150	$ -	$ 150	$ 150
Entertainment	$ 75	$ 75	$ -	$ 75	$ 75	$ -	$ 75	$ 75
Eating Out	$ 50	$ 50	$ -	$ 50	$ 50	$ -	$ 50	$ 50
Groceries	$ 325	$ 325	$ -	$ 325	$ 325	$ -	$ 325	$ 325
His Spending	$ 50	$ 50	$ -	$ 50	$ 50	$ -	$ 50	$ 50
Her Spending	$ 50	$ 50	$ -	$ 50	$ 50	$ -	$ 50	$ 50
Phone - House	$ 75	$ 75	$ -	$ 75	$ 75	$ -	$ 75	$ 75
Phone - Mobile	$ 65	$ 65	$ -	$ 65	$ 65	$ -	$ 65	$ 65
Subtotal	$ 1,040							
Periodic Required								
Auto Registration	$ 20	$ 20	$ -	$ 20	$ 20	$ -	$ 20	$ 20
Property Tax	$ 100	$ 100	$ -	$ 100	$ 100	$ -	$ 100	$ 100
Homeowner's Insurance	$ 75	$ 75	$ -	$ 75	$ 75	$ -	$ 75	$ 75
Life Insurance	$ 40	$ 40	$ -	$ 40	$ 40	$ -	$ 40	$ 40
Subtotal	$ 235							
Periodic Discretionary								
Medical Deductible	$ 55	$ 55	$ -	$ 55	$ 55	$ -	$ 55	$ 55
Birthday Gifts	$ 25	$ 25	$ -	$ 25	$ 25	$ -	$ 25	$ 25
Holiday Gifts	$ 70	$ -	$ 70	$ 140	$ 140	$ -	$ 70	$ 70
Auto Maintenance	$ 40	$ -	$ 40	$ 80	$ 60	$ 20	$ 60	$ 60
House Maintenance	$ 40	$ -	$ 40	$ 80	$ -	$ 80	$ 120	$ 120
Vacation	$ 150	$ -	$ 150	$ 300	$ -	$ 300	$ 450	$ 450
Subtotal	$ 380							
Total Net Monthly Income	$ 4,400	(a)$ 4,100	(b)$ 300	(c)$ 4,700	(d)$4,300	(e)$ 400	(f)$ 4,800	(g)$ 4,800

a) January paycheck was $4,100.
b) Monthly spending plan total is $4,400. Funding in January was $300 short.
c) The funding requirement for February is $4,400 plus $300 from January shortfall.
d) February paycheck was $4,300.
e) Monthly funding requirement for February is $4,700. Funding in February is $400 short.
f) The funding requirement for March is $4,400 plus $400 from February shortfall.
g) March paycheck is $4,800.

sions based on their bank account balances rather than their spending account balances.

If variable income is handled correctly within the envelope system, you can be very successful. If you plan wisely and spend prudently, you can benefit significantly from the upside potential that variable income can provide.

FIGURE C.3 ■ Defining Variable Income—Variable Period, Variable Amount

Defining Variable Income
Variable Period, Variable Amount

Variable Income Source	Pay Period	Net Amount Of Check	
ABC Corporation	January	$	7,800
	February	$	-
	March	$	4,800
	April	$	3,250
	May		
	June	$	9,350
	July		
	August	$	3,500
	September	$	7,200
	October	$	4,000
	November	$	3,700
	December	$	9,200
Total Annual Net Income		$	52,800
Average Monthly Net Income		$	4,400

FIGURE C.4 ■ Allocating Variable Income—Variable Period, Variable Amount

Allocating Variable Income
Variable Period, Variable Amount

Envelope Spending Accounts	Monthly Allocation Amount	January Allocations	Amount Underfunded	Month Two Funding Requirements	February Allocations	Amount Underfunded	Month Three Funding Requirements	March Allocations
Funding From Check		$ 7,800			$ -			$ 4,800
Funding From Savings		$ -			$ 3,400 (a)			$ -
Monthly Required								
Savings	$ 200	$ 200	$ -	$ 200	$ 200	$ -	$ 200	$ 200
Mortgage	$ 1,250	$ 1,250	$ -	$ 1,250	$ 1,250	$ -	$ 1,250	$ 1,250
Auto Loan	$ 375	$ 375	$ -	$ 375	$ 375	$ -	$ 375	$ 375
Credit Card # 1	$ 150	$ 150	$ -	$ 150	$ 150	$ -	$ 150	$ 150
Credit Card # 2	$ 75	$ 75	$ -	$ 75	$ 75	$ -	$ 75	$ 75
Auto Insurance	$ 120	$ 120	$ -	$ 120	$ 120	$ -	$ 120	$ 120
Power	$ 75	$ 75	$ -	$ 75	$ 75	$ -	$ 75	$ 75
Natural Gas	$ 65	$ 65	$ -	$ 65	$ 65	$ -	$ 65	$ 65
Water/Sewer/Garbage	$ 35	$ 35	$ -	$ 35	$ 35	$ -	$ 35	$ 35
Donations	$ 125	$ 125	$ -	$ 125	$ 125	$ -	$ 125	$ 125
Day Care	$ 275	$ 275	$ -	$ 275	$ 275	$ -	$ 275	$ 275
Subtotal	$ 2,745							
Monthly Discretionary								
Auto Fuel	$ 175	$ 175	$ -	$ 175	$ 175	$ -	$ 175	$ 175
Babysitter	$ 25	$ 25	$ -	$ 25	$ 20	$ 5	$ 30	$ 30
Clothing	$ 150	$ 150	$ -	$ 150	$ 35	$ 115	$ 265	$ 265
Entertainment	$ 75	$ 75	$ -	$ 75	$ 50	$ 25	$ 100	$ 100
Eating Out	$ 50	$ 50	$ -	$ 50	$ 50	$ -	$ 50	$ 50
Groceries	$ 325	$ 325	$ -	$ 325	$ 325	$ -	$ 325	$ 325
His Spending	$ 50	$ 50	$ -	$ 50	$ -	$ 50	$ 100	$ 100
Her Spending	$ 50	$ 50	$ -	$ 50	$ -	$ 50	$ 100	$ 100
Phone - House	$ 75	$ 75	$ -	$ 75	$ -	$ 75	$ 150	$ 150
Phone - Mobile	$ 65	$ 65	$ -	$ 65	$ -	$ 65	$ 130	$ 130
Subtotal	$ 1,040							
Periodic Required								
Auto Registration	$ 20	$ 20	$ -	$ 20	$ -	$ 20	$ 40	$ 40
Property Tax	$ 100	$ 100	$ -	$ 100	$ -	$ 100	$ 200	$ 200
Homeowner's Insurance	$ 75	$ 75	$ -	$ 75	$ -	$ 75	$ 150	$ 150
Life Insurance	$ 40	$ 40	$ -	$ 40	$ -	$ 40	$ 80	$ 80
Subtotal	$ 235							
Periodic Discretionary								
Medical Deductible	$ 55	$ 55	$ -	$ 55	$ -	$ 55	$ 110	$ 110
Birthday Gifts	$ 25	$ 25	$ -	$ 25	$ -	$ 25	$ 50	$ 50
Holiday Gifts	$ 70	$ 70	$ -	$ 70	$ -	$ 70	$ 140	
Auto Maintenance	$ 40	$ 40	$ -	$ 40	$ -	$ 40	$ 80	$ -
House Maintenance	$ 40	$ 40	$ -	$ 40	$ -	$ 40	$ 80	$ -
Vacation	$ 150	$ 150	$ -	$ 150	$ -	$ 150	$ 300	$ -
Subtotal	$ 380							
Total Net Monthly Income	$ 4,400	$ 4,400	$ -	$ 4,400	$ 3,400 (b)	$ 1,000	$ 5,400	$ 4,800
Savings Account for Income Holding								
Beginning Balance		$ -			$ 3,400			$ -
Deposits		$ 3,400			$ -			$ -
Withdrawals		$ -			$ 3,400			$ -
Ending Balance		$ 3,400			$ -			$ -

a) No paycheck in February. $3,400 transferred from holding account to cover funding requirements for February.

b) Holding account balance is zero after February funding.

Appendix D ■
Reference Material

Money *for Life* and Mvelopes® Personal are your key components to understanding and implementing an envelope system. These two items may be all of the resources you need to achieve financial fitness. However, you may require additional assistance in certain areas to ensure your success, and there are a number of resources available to assist you. The information below is a compilation of sources that you can access for education, planning, or coaching.

■ READING LIST

- *The Millionaire Next Door,* by Thomas J. Stanley, Ph.D., and William D. Danko, Ph.D. (Pocket Books, 1998)
- *You Don't Have to Be Rich,* by Jean Chatzky (Portfolio, 2003)
- *Talking Money,* by Jean Chatzky (Warner Business, 2002)
- *The Richest Man in Babylon,* by George S. Clason (Signet Reissue, 2004)
- *The Budget Kit,* 4th ed., by Judy Lawrence (Dearborn Trade, 2004)
- *Rich on Any Income,* by James P. Christensen and Clint Combs with George D. Durrant (Bookcraft Publications, 1986)
- *Just Give Me the Answers,* by Sheryl Garrett (Dearborn Trade, 2004)
- *The Total Money Makeover,* by Dave Ramsey (Thomas Nelson, 2003)
- *The 9 Steps to Financial Freedom,* by Suze Orman (Three Rivers Press, 2000)
- *Get a Financial Life,* by Beth Kobliner (Fireside, 2000)

- *Your Money or Your Life,* by Joe Dominguez and Vicki Robin (Penguin USA, 1999)
- *The Complete Cheapskate,* by Mary Hunt (St. Martin's Press, 2003)

WEB SITE RESOURCES

- Mvelopes® Resource Page (http://www.mvelopes.com/resources). Compilation of education, financial planning, and coaching resources
- Personal Finance Budgeting (http://www.personalfinancebudgeting.com)
- Smart Money Tips (http://www.smartmoneytips.com)
- My Online Bill Pay (http://www.myonlinebillpay.com)
- Garrett Planning Network: Financial Planners (http://www.garrettplanningnetwork.com)
- The Money Tracker (http://www.moneytracker.com)
- The Total Money Makeover (http://www.daveramsey.com)
- The Frugal Shopper (http://www.thefrugalshopper.com)
- Lower My Bills (http://www.lowermybills.com)
- The Dollar Stretcher (http://www.stretcher.com)
- CNN MONEY: Money 101 (http://www.money.cnn.com/pf/101)
- Money Watchers (http://www.moneywatchers.biz)
- Mvelopes Resource Page: Debt Calculator (http://www.mvelopes.com/debt_calculator)
- Bankrate Financial Calculators (http://www.bankrate.com/brm/rate/calc_home.asp)
- Cardweb Credit Card Statistics (http://www.cardweb.com)
- CNN MONEY Calculators (http://cgi.money.cnn.com/tools)
- Moneyspot (http://www.moneyspot.org)
- Womens Wall Street (http://womenswallstreet.com)
- Womens Wall Street Calculators (http://womenswallstreet.com/wws/calculators.aspx?titleid=9)
- Java Financial Calculators (http://dinkytown.net)

RECOMMENDED ENVELOPES AND SPENDING PERCENTAGES

FIGURE D.1 ■ Recommended Spending Percentages

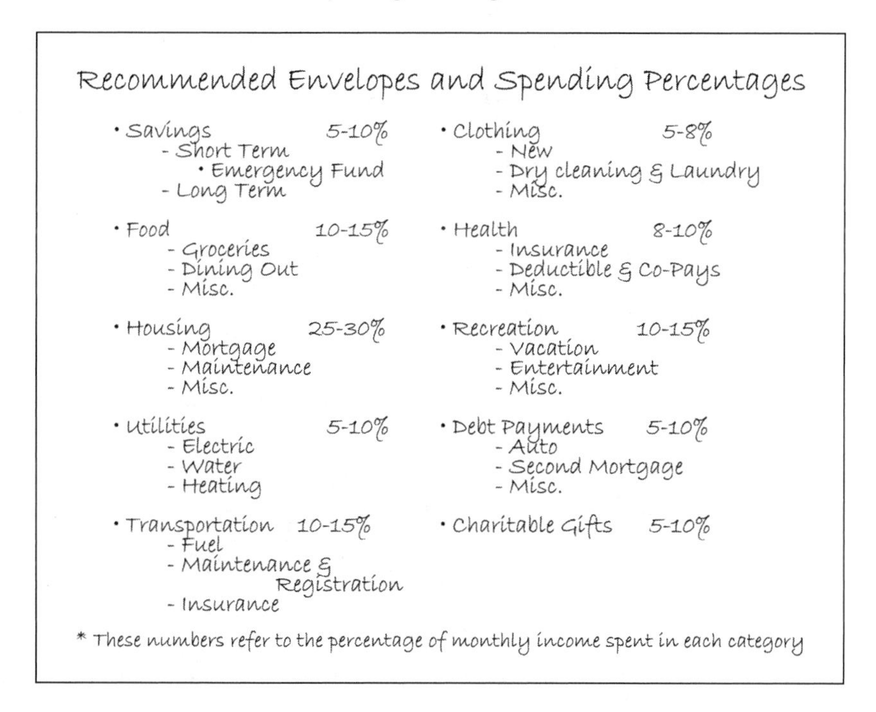

DEBT CALCULATORS AND REPORTS

One of the most important elements in achieving financial fitness is to eliminate debt so that your income can be used productively to achieve your goals. The following debt reports and calculators will provide you with the information you need to develop your debt elimination plan and track progress to meet your goals. (See Figures D.2 and D.3.)

FIGURE D.2 ■ Debt Calculator Report

Debt Calculator Report

Mvelopes Personal can:
- Save you up to **$123,450** in interest
- Reduce your debt pay-off time by **13 years 2 months**
- No Accelerator

Your Current Debt Pay-off
Based on the debt information you've provided, your total current debt pay-off summary is:
Total pay-off time: 26 years 10 months **Total interest paid: $265,641**

Using Mvelopes Personal
Using Mvelopes Personal and applying debt roll-down, your debt pay-off summary is:
Total pay-off time: 13 years 8 months **Total interest paid: $142,191**

Debt Summary

Loan Type	Amount Owed	Interest Rate	Monthly Payment
Dept. Store	$435	21%	$75
Credit Card	$4,350	18.5%	$95
Credit Card	$4,855	14.5%	$75
Auto Loan	$14,750	8.9%	$517
Other	$9,875	8.5%	$142
Other	$3,950	7.5%	$142
Mortgage	$206,320	7%	$1,422
Total	**$244,535**		**$2,468**

1. Dept. Store	Loan Amount	Interest Paid	Pay-off Time
Current pay-off	$435	$28	6 months
Mvelopes pay-off	$435	$28	6 months
Using Mvelopes	Time Saved:		
	Interest Saved: $0		

2. Credit Card	Loan Amount	Interest Paid	Pay-off Time
Current pay-off	$4,350	$3,250	6 years 8 months
Mvelopes pay-off	$4,350	$1,516	3 years 1 month
Using Mvelopes	Time Saved: 3 years 7 months		
	Interest Saved: $1,734		

3. Credit Card	Loan Amount	Interest Paid	Pay-off Time
Current pay-off	$4,855	$4,662	10 years 7 months
Mvelopes pay-off	$4,855	$4,662	4 years 8 months
Using Mvelopes	Time Saved: 5 years 11 months		
	Interest Saved: $2,126		

4. Auto Loan	Loan Amount	Interest Paid	Pay-off Time
Current pay-off	$14,750	$1,884	2 years 8 months
Mvelopes pay-off	$14,750	$0	1 year 9 months
Using Mvelopes	Time Saved: 11 months		
	Interest Saved: $1,884		

5. Other	Loan Amount	Interest Paid	Pay-off Time
Current pay-off	$9,875	$3,774	8 years
Mvelopes pay-off	$9,875	$3,137	5 years 2 months
Using Mvelopes	Time Saved: 2 years 11 months		
	Interest Saved: $637		

6. Other	Loan Amount	Interest Paid	Pay-off Time
Current pay-off	$3,950	$403	2 years 7 months
Mvelopes pay-off	$3,950	$403	2 years 7 months
Using Mvelopes	Time Saved:		
	Interest Saved: $0		

7. Mortgage	Loan Amount	Interest Paid	Pay-off Time
Current pay-off	$206,320	$251,640	26 years 10 months
Mvelopes pay-off	$206,320	$134,571	13 years 8 months
Using Mvelopes	Time Saved: 13 years 2 months		
	Interest Saved: $117,069		

FIGURE D.3 ■ Debt Calculator Report with Accelerator

Debt Calculator Report With Accelerator

Mvelopes Personal can:
- Save you up to **$179,424** in interest
- Reduce your debt pay-off time by **17 years 11 months**
- Accelerator= $624 per month

Your Current Debt Pay-off
Based on the debt information you've provided, your total current debt pay-off summary is:
Total pay-off time: 26 years 10 months **Total interest paid: $265,641**

Using Mvelopes Personal
Using Mvelopes Personal and applying debt roll-down, your debt pay-off summary is:
Total pay-off time: 8 years 11 months **Total interest paid: $86,217**

Debt Summary

Loan Type	Amount Owed	Interest Rate	Monthly Payment
Dept. Store	$435	21%	$75
Credit Card	$4,350	18.5%	$95
Credit Card	$4,855	14.5%	$75
Auto Loan	$14,750	8.9%	$517
Other	$9,875	8.5%	$142
Other	$3,950	7.5%	$142
Mortgage	$206,320	7%	$1,422
Total	**$244,535**		**$2,468**

1. Dept. Store	Loan Amount	Interest Paid	Pay-off Time
Current pay-off	$435	$28	6 months
Mvelopes pay-off	$435	$6	1 month
Using Mvelopes	Time Saved: 6 months Interest Saved: $22		

2. Credit Card	Loan Amount	Interest Paid	Pay-off Time
Current pay-off	$4,350	$3,250	6 years 8 months
Mvelopes pay-off	$4,350	$270	6 month
Using Mvelopes	Time Saved: 6 years 2 months Interest Saved: $2,980		

3. Credit Card	Loan Amount	Interest Paid	Pay-off Time
Current pay-off	$4,855	$4,662	10 years 7 months
Mvelopes pay-off	$4,855	$564	1 year
Using Mvelopes	Time Saved: 9 years 7 months Interest Saved: $4,098		

4. Auto Loan	Loan Amount	Interest Paid	Pay-off Time
Current pay-off	$14,750	$1,884	2 years 8 months
Mvelopes pay-off	$14,750	$1,406	1 year 7 months
Using Mvelopes	Time Saved: 1 year 1 month Interest Saved: $478		

5. Other	Loan Amount	Interest Paid	Pay-off Time
Current pay-off	$9,875	$3,774	8 years
Mvelopes pay-off	$9,875	$1,449	2 years 1 month
Using Mvelopes	Time Saved: 5 years 11 months Interest Saved: $2,325		

6. Other	Loan Amount	Interest Paid	Pay-off Time
Current pay-off	$3,950	$403	2 years 7 months
Mvelopes pay-off	$3,950	$389	2 years 1 month
Using Mvelopes	Time Saved: 5 months Interest Saved: $14		

7. Mortgage	Loan Amount	Interest Paid	Pay-off Time
Current pay-off	$206,320	$251,640	26 years 10 months
Mvelopes pay-off	$206,320	$82,133	8 years 11 months
Using Mvelopes	Time Saved: 17 years 11 months Interest Saved: $169,507		

Appendix E ■ Mvelopes® Personal: An Envelope System for Today's World

Mvelopes® Personal is a tool being used by thousands to successfully implement the envelope principles on a daily basis. When Tom met with Ryan and Christine, he introduced them to a computer and Internet-based system that automated the envelope process. This was very important to them because of the complexities associated with managing finances in today's world. As our society becomes less dependent on traditional forms of payment and more focused on cashless spending tools, it is important to utilize a tool that will allow you to create a context for decision making by appropriately incorporating all types of spending from all types of accounts.

At the back of this book you will find a CD containing the setup information necessary to utilize the Mvelopes Personal system. This system has been provided to you to use risk-free for 30 days. To begin using Mvelopes Personal, simply insert the CD into the CD-ROM drive of your computer and follow the activation instructions. If no CD has been included, please go to http://www.mvelopes.com/moneyforlife to get more information.

Mvelopes Personal will allow you to successfully implement the envelope concepts outlined in this book. As you begin using the system, it will assist you with defining your initial spending plan, automatically track all of your transactions, automatically update your envelope spending account balances, and allow you to make timely and appropriate adjustments.

A brief description of the key features and benefits of the Mvelopes Personal system follows.

EASILY CREATE A BUDGET: YOUR SPENDING PLAN

Mvelopes Personal allows you to simply and easily define your monthly income and then set up spending accounts, or envelopes, to which you allocate that income. When you receive a paycheck, Mvelopes lets you split the amount between the various spending accounts you have set up. Spending categories are completely up to you. You can create as many envelopes as you need, and you can group them under category headings as you see fit. For example, the automobile expenses group may contain envelopes for gasoline, repairs, and insurance. By creating envelopes for periodic expenses, such as vacations, car registration fees, or an emergency fund, you can set aside money today for your future spending requirements. Setting a portion of your income aside each month will mean that the money will be there when periodic expenses are incurred, so you do not have to increase your debt to meet these spending requirements.

MANAGE YOUR SPENDING WITH ANYTIME, ANYWHERE ACCESS TO YOUR BUDGET

A real advantage to Mvelopes Personal is that it is an online budgeting system, which means you are not tied to your home computer. You and your partner can have anytime, anywhere access to your budget through the Mvelopes secure online service. This means both of you can be looking at your daily spending activity at the same time—at work, at home, on the road, or anywhere you have Internet access. As with Ryan and Christine, when you both stay involved in the budgeting process, you can count on being successful. Mvelopes allows you to securely and easily access your information from anywhere, providing you with the ability to make informed spending decisions. (See Figure E.1.)

FIGURE E.1 ■ Mvelopes® Personal Home Screen

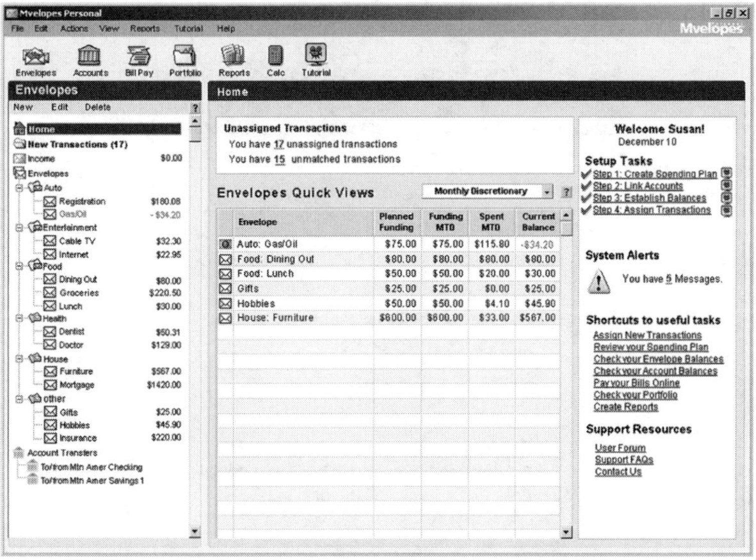

■ EASILY TRACK ALL YOUR SPENDING

Mvelopes Personal retrieves all your spending and deposit transactions on a daily basis, automatically, from your bank, credit union, or credit card company, bringing all your transactions into one place for you to see. (See Figure E.2 for an example.)

The interaction you have with each transaction makes managing your spending easy. Mvelopes retrieves each of your transactions from all of your online banking and credit accounts. Each transaction is assigned to an envelope, where the expense is deducted from the income that you allocated to that envelope. You will then be able to see your balance and know exactly how much you have left to spend in each envelope spending account. By always knowing exactly how much you have left to spend, you can make better spending decisions. (See Figure E.3.)

FIGURE E.2 ■ Mvelopes® Personal New Transactions Screen

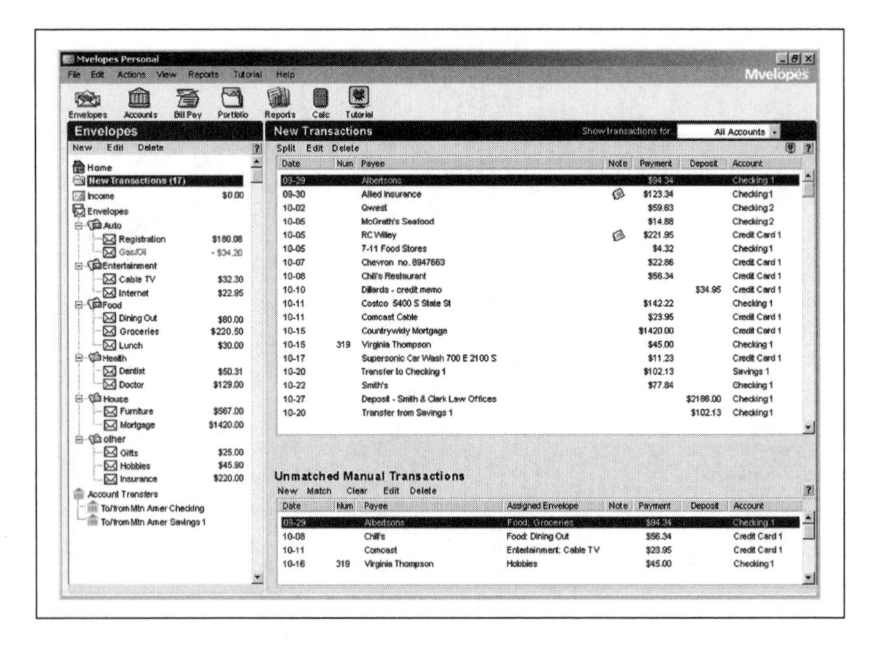

FIGURE E.3 ■ Mvelopes® Personal Envelope Register Screen

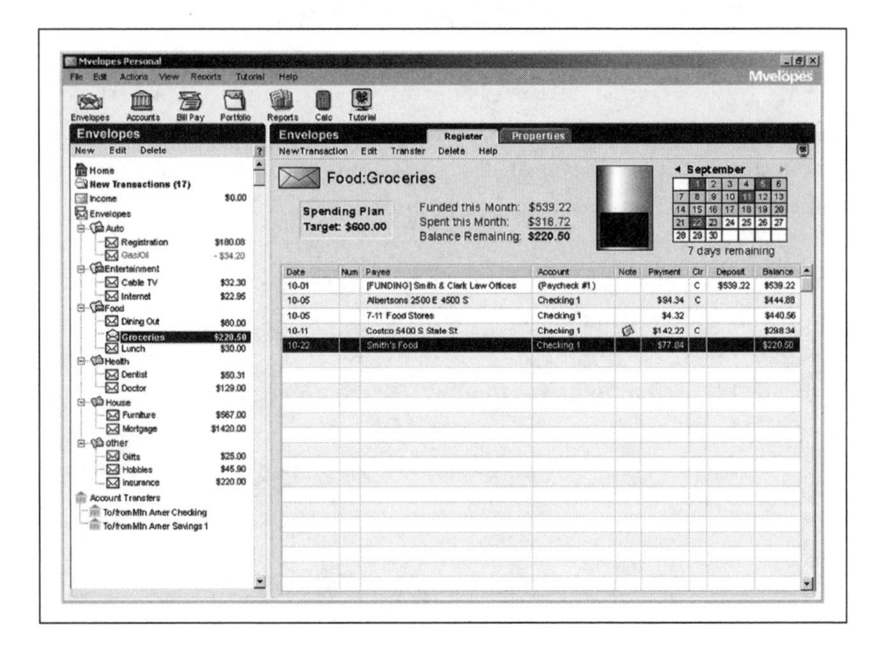

RECOVER UP TO 20 PERCENT OF YOUR INCOME FROM HIDDEN SPENDING

By knowing where your money is going using the Mvelopes Personal unique approach to spending management, you will be able to recover between 10 and 20 percent of your income from hidden spending. All those little purchases can add up to more than you realize! With better tracking and forecasting, you can recover that money. For example, over the course of a year, based on a $40,000 salary, 10 percent would be an extra $4,000 to use for debt reduction, savings, or investments.

AUTOMATICALLY PAY ALL YOUR BILLS ONLINE

Included with Mvelopes Personal is a complete online bill payment service—no more writing checks, licking stamps, or going to the post office. Payments can be made manually, set up for automatic payment each month, or with the arrival of an electronic bill. The service allows you up to 20 payments a month, which could save you more than $7 a month in postage alone. Payments can be made to any company, store, financial institution, utility company, or individual, eliminating missed payments and late fees. (See Figure E.4.)

EFFECTIVELY MANAGE CREDIT CARD SPENDING WITHOUT ADDING ADDITIONAL DEBT

In today's society, credit cards are often used as an income source instead of a convenient spending tool. Consequently, there is usually no income available at the end of the month to pay off the debt. Mvelopes manages credit card purchasing by automatically moving allocated funds from your spending envelopes to a credit card repayment envelope every time you use your card. Here's how it works: When you use your credit card to pay for dinner at a local restaurant, that transaction is received into Mvelopes and assigned to your dining out envelope. That amount is then deducted from the dining out envelope and placed into your credit card repayment envelope. (See Figure E.5.)

FIGURE E.4 ■ Mvelopes® Personal Bill Pay Screen

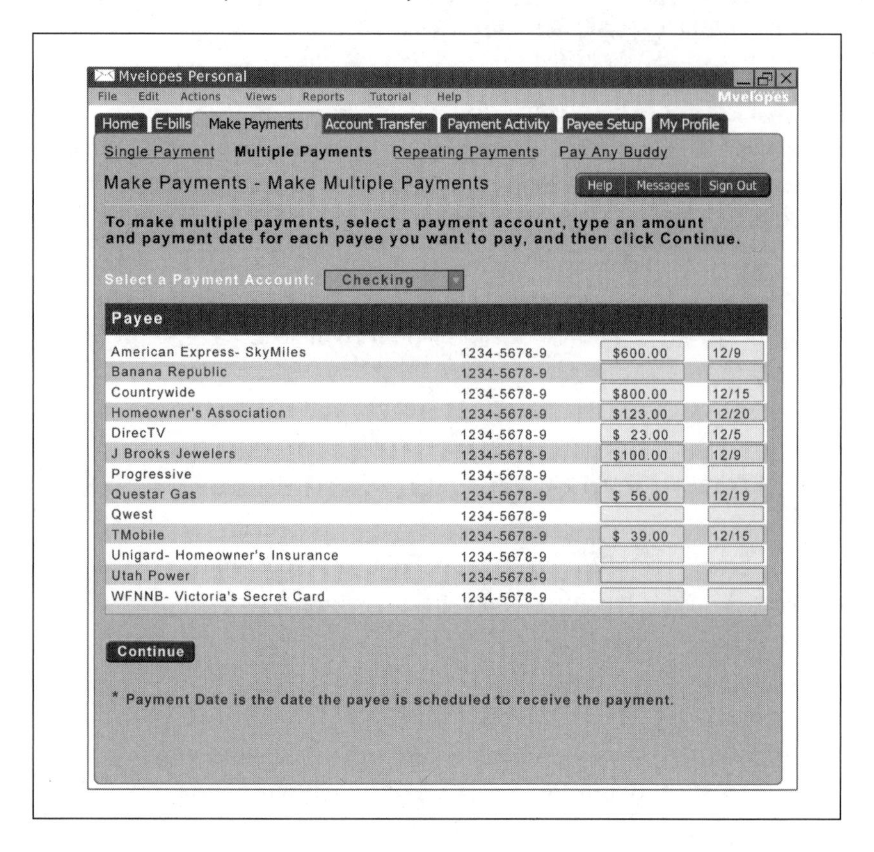

FIGURE E.5 ■ Mvelopes® Personal Credit Card Tracking

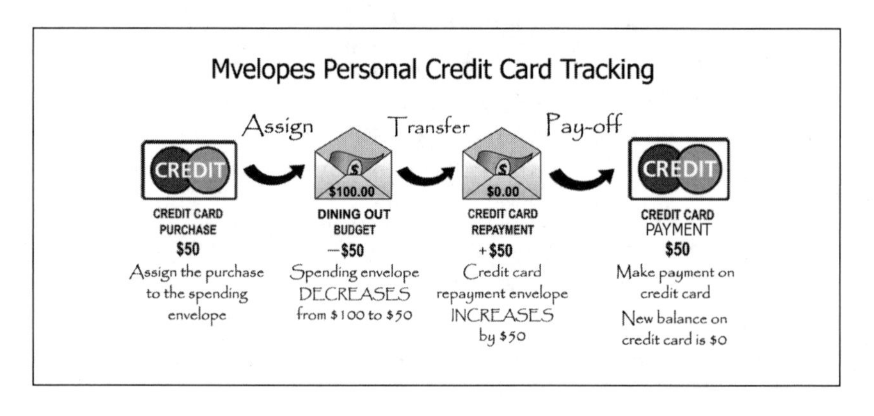

At the end of the month, you will have money set aside to pay off your credit card in full—no additional debt incurred and no outrageous interest payments.

QUICKLY ELIMINATE DEBT

Mvelopes users have found that by managing their spending closely, they are able to eliminate overspending and even save extra money each month. In many cases, there will be money left in several of your discretionary envelopes at the end of the month. By sweeping those extra amounts into current debt payments, you can quickly eliminate your debt.

If you have more than one debt, when that first debt is paid in full, you can roll that whole payment amount plus the extra into your next priority debt on the list (see debt roll-down in Applied Principle 15, page 116). Once you are debt free, you can roll those former debt payments into savings and investments to provide a more financially stable future for yourself and your family.

MANAGE YOUR COMPLETE PORTFOLIO

Track all of your investments from Mportfolio™, so that you can see the big picture from one summary page. As an integral part of your Mvelopes Personal budgeting system, you can customize Mportfolio to access and track all of your investment accounts, such as IRAs, 401(k)s, and mutual funds. This summary page allows you to see your complete financial picture in one quick snapshot, rather than surfing around to several different sites to see the balances in all your varying accounts. (See Figure E.6.) Should you want to make changes to an account, you can simply click on that account to access the screen where you can make the appropriate adjustments.

GENERATE CLEAR, INFORMATIVE REPORTS

With Mvelopes Personal, you can generate any number of reports that will help you see where you are in your quest to become financially

FIGURE E.6 ■ Mvelopes® Personal Mportfolio™ Screen

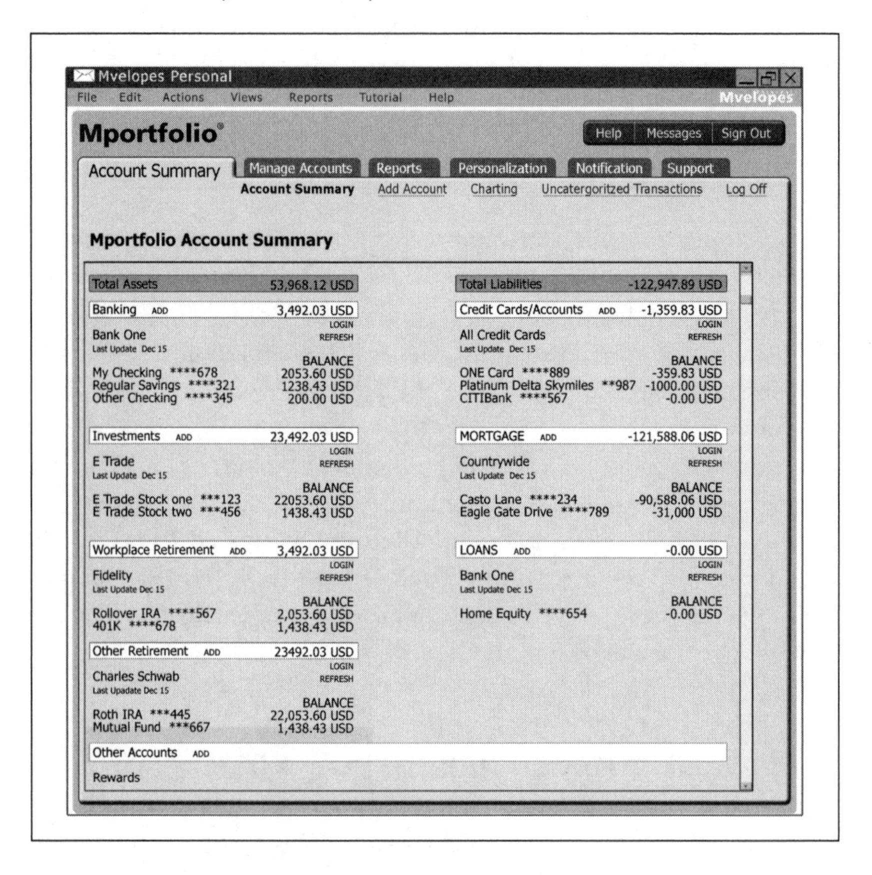

fit. These reports make everything easier, from doing your taxes, to planning a special event, or even just reviewing your financial status. (See Figure E.7.) Reports can be generated in numerous ways:

- Search for transactions by payee or by date.
- Review transactions or envelope registers for a certain day, week, or month.
- Calculate what portion of your expenses are in a particular category.
- Compare income allocation against actual expenses for any envelope category by day, month, and year.
- View the current status of your envelopes and accounts with the monthly allocation, balance, and current spending.

FIGURE E.7 ■ Mvelopes® Personal Summary Report

Mvelopes Summary Report

Group Name	Mvelope Name	Monthly allocation	Spent this month	Current balance
	Childcare	$180.00	$0.00	$180.00
	Clothing	$150.00	$56.25	$93.75
	Donations	$30.00	$0.00	$30.00
	Household	$100.00	$0.00	$100.00
	Miscellaneous	$50.00	$0.00	$50.00
	Savings	$408.17	$0.00	$408.17
Allowances	Me	$50.00	$0.00	$50.00
	Spouse	$50.00	$0.00	$50.00
Auto	Gas & Oil	$133.00	$25.00	$108.00
	Registration	$33.33	$0.00	$166.69
Debt/Payments To	American Express	$0.00	$23.87	$123.87
	Citibank VISA	$60.00	$0.00	$60.00
Debts	Car Payments	$630.00	$0.00	$630.00
	Mortgage	$1,200.00	$0.00	$1,200.00
Entertainment	Cable & Internet	$50.00	$0.00	$50.00
	Movies/Events	$125.00	$8.10	$116.90
Financial Plan	College Fund	$50.00	$0.00	$50.00
	IRA	$100.00	$0.00	$100.00
	Investments	$100.00	$0.00	$100.00
Food	Dining Out	$140.00	$23.87	$116.13
	Groceries	$415.00	$0.00	$415.00
Health	Co-Pay/Supplies	$75.00	$0.00	$75.00
Insurance	Auto	$100.00	$0.00	$500.00
	Health	$100.00	$0.00	$100.00
	Housing	$41.00	$0.00	$41.00
	Life	$110.00	$0.00	$110.00
System	Monthly Funding	$0.00	$0.00	$979.14
	Shortfall	$0.00	$0.00	$0.00
Taxes	Property Taxes	$100.00	$0.00	$100.00
Utilities	Electricity	$111.00	$0.00	$111.00
	Gas	$36.00	$0.00	$36.00
	Mobile Phone	$50.00	$0.00	$50.00
	Phone	$72.00	$0.00	$72.00
	Water	$38.00	$0.00	$38.00
Totals		**$4,887.50**	**$137.09**	**$6,410.65**

■ RECEIVE UNLIMITED CUSTOMER SUPPORT AND BUDGET COACHING

Included with your Mvelopes Personal online service is unlimited telephone support and coaching, as well as access to our message boards, FAQs, tutorials, and e-mail support. Members also receive a monthly online newsletter with tips for using the Mvelopes system and other useful financial fitness suggestions.

AUTOMATIC FEATURE UPGRADES AT NO ADDITIONAL COST

Any upgrades to the Mvelopes Personal online budgeting system are included free of charge to all Mvelopes members—no more worrying about paying for and upgrading to the next version of software.

IN SUMMARY

For additional information, please visit http://www.mvelopes.com. If you are looking for a financial advisor, educator, or coach who understands the Mvelopes Personal system and would like contact information, please to go to http://www.mvelopes.com/resources and simply find the resource most suited to your needs.